Mushrooms and Truffles of the Southwest

D1554775

Hygrophorus speciosus

Mushrooms and Truffles of the Southwest

JACK S. STATES

Published with the assistance of
Transition Zone Horticultural Institute, Inc.
The Arboretum at Flagstaff

THE UNIVERSITY OF ARIZONA PRESS   TUCSON

Transition Zone Horticultural Institute, Inc.

THE ARBORETUM AT FLAGSTAFF

This book was published with the assistance of The Arboretum at Flagstaff, a nonprofit institution, which was established in 1981 as a center for plant research and public exhibition. Located southwest of Flagstaff, Arizona, the Arboretum occupies two hundred acres of ponderosa pine forest land. At an elevation of 7,150 feet, it is the highest arboretum in the United States doing horticultural research. Through integrated programs of plant collections, research, and public education, it studies and disseminates information concerning horticulture that is appropriate for the dry, high elevation communities of the West.

Neither the author nor the publisher accepts responsibility for the reader's identifications of mushrooms and truffles or the consequences of eating any of the fungi listed in this book.

The University of Arizona Press
Copyright © 1990
The Arizona Board of Regents
All Rights Reserved
Printed in Japan
Set in Linotron 202 Sabon.
♾ This book is printed on acid-free, archival-quality paper.
Manufactured in the United States of America.

94 93 92 91 90   5 4 3 2 1

LIBRARY OF CONGRESS CATALOGING-IN-PUBLICATION DATA
States, Jack S., 1941–
    Mushrooms and truffles of the Southwest / Jack S. States.
    p. cm.
    Includes bibliographical references.
    ISBN 0-8165-1162-4 (alk. paper). — ISBN (invalid) 0-8165-1182-6
(pbk. : alk. paper)
1. Fungi—Southwest, New—Identification. 2. Fungi—Mexico—
Identification. 3. Truffles—Southwest, New—Identification.
4. Truffles—Mexico—Identification. I. Title.
QK605.5.S683S73   1990
589.2'0979—dc20   89-20693
                                                        CIP

I dedicate this book with love to Diantha,
with whom I share the wonder, the search, and the discovery.

Contents

Special Features of This Publication   9

Introduction   11

  Southwestern Fungi and Their Environment   13

    Characteristics of Fungi and Lichens   16

    Edible and Poisonous Fungi   18

    Life Zones of the Southwest   19

Collection and Identification of Fungi   23

  Collection Suggestions   23

  Fungus Classification   24

  How to Use the Keys   25

  Cross-References   27

Picture Key to the Major Groups of Fungi and Fungus Relatives   29

Narrative Key to the Major Groups of Fungi and Fungus Relatives   36

Club Fungi

BASIDIOMYCETES   41

  Fleshy Gilled and Fleshy Pored Fungi: Order Agaricales   42

    Key to the Major Families of the Agaricales   42

  Aphyllophorales-Cantharelloid, Coral, Toothed, Crust and
Woody-Pored Fungi   121

    Key to the Cantharelloid, Coral, Toothed, and Woody-Pored
Aphyllophorales   123

Jelly Fungi: Tremellales and Auriculariales   142

Stomach Fungi
GASTEROMYCETES   146
   Puffballs and Allies and Agaricoid Gasteromycetes   146
      Key to Selected Gasteromycetes   147

Sac Fungi
ASCOMYCETES   171
   Cup Fungi, Saddle Fungi, and Morels   171
      Key to the Ascomycetes   172

Truffles and False Truffles
TUBERLIKE ASCOMYCETES AND BASIDIOMYCETES   186
      Key to the Tuberlike Fungi   187

Slime Molds
MYXOMYCETES   204

Lichens   207

Glossary   215

Bibliography   219

Index   221

Photograph Credits   233

Figures
1   Map of Vegetational Zones of the Southwest   14–15
2   Life Zones of the Southwest   20

Special Features of This Publication

This is the first publication of its kind to cover the broad range of fungi and fungus relatives found in the American Southwest. Emphasis is placed on mushrooms and truffles most commonly encountered in this region, but selected slime molds and lichens are also included.

The geographic scope includes Arizona, New Mexico, and parts of Colorado, Utah, Nevada, California, and northern Mexico.

The reader is directed to the particular life zone where the fungi can be found in association with characteristic plant communities. Therefore, the natural history of mushrooms is emphasized. Maps are included to illustrate major life zones, particularly conifer forests where mushrooms are most frequently found on public land. Major landmarks, including cities, highways, and mountain ranges, are provided.

Keys lead to descriptions and corresponding color illustrations for 156 of the major mushroom and truffle species. Additional descriptive references for 155 other species are included. An extremely useful and unique feature of this guide is the provision of cross-references to other mushroom field guides that contain additional color illustrations and descriptions of many of the fungi listed. No serious mushroom hunter should rely on a single reference for identification, especially if the intent is to consume the mushroom. A bibliography of references and suggested readings has been provided.

An attempt has been made to keep scientific terminology to a minimum. Terms of special significance have been italicized in the text and are defined in the glossary. Notations on toxicity and edibility are provided.

Introduction

"Nature alone is antique and the oldest art a mushroom"
—CARLYLE

"Spectacular," "bizarre," "delightful," and "mysterious" are common expletives applied to the discovery of mushrooms. Mushrooms are neither plant nor animal. They are the reproductive bodies of fungi that typically appear above ground in forests and meadows, and they are just as numerous and varied as flowering plants. The wide range of shape, size, and color attracts the attention of artist and naturalist alike. They make a most fascinating study and their popularity is ever increasing. We often come to know mushrooms by their reputation, whether as a gourmet delight or as poisonous and deadly. Although relatively few in number, the poisonous varieties provide strong encouragement for us to know them well. In addition to the enjoyment of hunting and the pleasure of new mushroom discoveries, the cryptic association of fungi with the decaying dead lends to the search a certain mystique that inspires the avid *fungiphile*.

There are many fungi that have not been adequately studied, just as there are new *species* that await discovery. Truffles, hidden to all but those with an educated eye and keen sense of smell, are an equally interesting and diverse group of fungi whose fruiting bodies rarely appear above ground. Because of their *hypogeous* (subterranean) habitat, the challenge of their discovery is all the more exciting. Few of these fungi have been described in mushroom guides, yet they are abundant in our southwestern *deciduous hardwood* and *coniferous* forests. They offer a "new frontier" to the mushroom hunter.

As amateur and professional collectors we are aware that proper identification is essential in order to suitably study and appreciate the myriad of mushrooms and truffles discovered thus far. Only recently have popular books, adequate for their identification, become available. Still, the bewildering array of different fungi presented in these guides poses a significant challenge to those who attempt to identify them. It is perhaps fortunate that despite the potential for hundreds of fungus species to occur simultaneously in a given area, they are instead, quite selective as to where and when to grow. For example, many fungi prefer to grow in association with particular kinds of trees and other perennial plants. These plants are often found in distinctive combinations within well defined geographic regions called *life zones* or biotic communities. Because the associated fungi also form recognizable communities, one can predict their occurrence within the life zone.

This book is written with the purpose of describing mushrooms and truffles common to the American Southwest. Because it is a guide that focuses on the fungal community, or *mycoflora*, of a region, it can treat a smaller percentage of mushrooms and truffles that are typical of the area as well as verify the occurrence of some of the best known and widely distributed species. It is not the intent of this guide to provide complete coverage of the mushrooms and truffles found in the Southwest but rather to present a selection of those that, in combination, are distinctive and common to the life zones of this region. Fourteen major groups are described; two groups, the slime molds and the lichens, are not specifically fungi but are funguslike in appearance. Selected representative *lichens* are introduced here, not only because they are a combined fungus-alga association, but also because they are widespread and abundant in the arid environments of the Southwest. This is the first presentation of lichens in a book of this kind.

Many of the frequently encountered mushroom species are also widely distributed. This is true of their plant hosts as well. Therefore, familiarity with vascular plant identities is a valuable aid in the hunting and identification of fungi. Equally important is a knowledge of the environmental and seasonal factors that influence the occurrence of mushrooms within each plant community. A chapter describing the life zones of the Southwest and their environmental characteristics is included. Reference to these habitats is made in the species descriptions and in the checklist of southwestern fungi. Much of the practical information on mushrooms, such as edibility, host association, and seasonal fruiting, has been contributed by nonspecialists. The reader of this book will have an opportunity to make new discoveries that go beyond the scope of these pages. Just as in other disciplines of natural history, local and national organizations exist to share information on mycological topics. New discoveries can be added to the growing body of mycological knowledge by lay persons and discussed with experts in nearby colleges, universities, and mycological societies.

SOUTHWESTERN FUNGI AND THEIR ENVIRONMENT

The American Southwest, because of its unique geographic position, experiences extremes of climate and season found nowhere else in the northern hemisphere. Ultra-blue skies, spectacular sunsets, torrential thundershowers, mountain blizzards, scorching deserts, and blinding sandstorms highlight, within a single season, the environmental setting in which various forms of fungi are found. Situated in a general way between 28 and 38°N latitude and between 102 and 118°W longitude, this region is geologically and biologically diverse. It is not surprising that many people consider the Southwest a desert. It encompasses portions of the Great Basin cool desert as well as parts of the vast Sonoran, Mohave, and Chihuahuan hot deserts. Actually, over one hundred million acres of forest are present including the southern end of the Rocky Mountains and northern portions of the Sierra Madre Occidental in Mexico (see Figure 1). Much of the Southwest in the United States is public land managed by the federal government in eight national parks, sixteen national monuments, and fifteen national forests. The majority of mushroom and truffle species are associated with coniferous and deciduous forest trees. Many of these fungi form *mycorrhizae*, a mutually beneficial association of the fungus *mycelium* with tree roots. As described later in the text, mycorrhizal fungi do not grow in the absence of their host associate. Therefore, each forest type supports a distinctive mycoflora, which in turn is different from the mycofloras found in scrublands, grasslands, and deserts. The low-elevation conifer forests, comprised primarily of pine and juniper species, predominate in the mountainous regions of northern Mexico, New Mexico, Arizona, and the southern parts of Utah and Colorado. Alpine tundra and subalpine forests occur in disjunct, islandlike promontories as remnants of the more extensive forests in the northern Rocky Mountains. There is overlap of adjacent water-dependent Riparian deciduous forest and woodland plant communities but these are much less expansive than those of the western and eastern United States. The mycofloras of the Great Plains grasslands of eastern New Mexico and western Texas, and the evergreen woodlands and

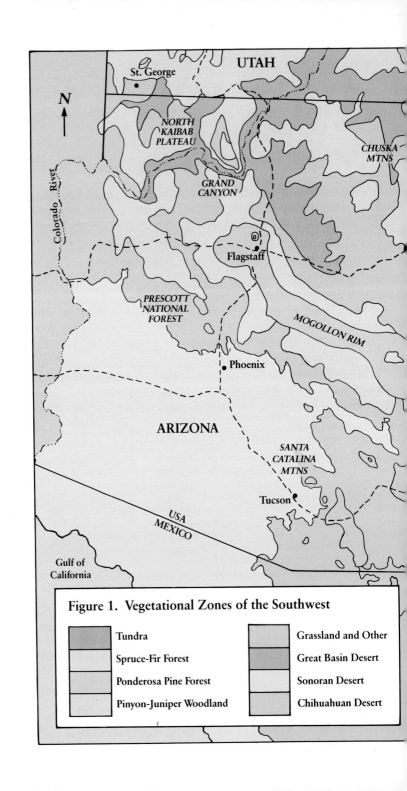

Figure 1. Vegetational Zones of the Southwest

Tundra

Spruce-Fir Forest

Ponderosa Pine Forest

Pinyon-Juniper Woodland

Grassland and Other

Great Basin Desert

Sonoran Desert

Chihuahuan Desert

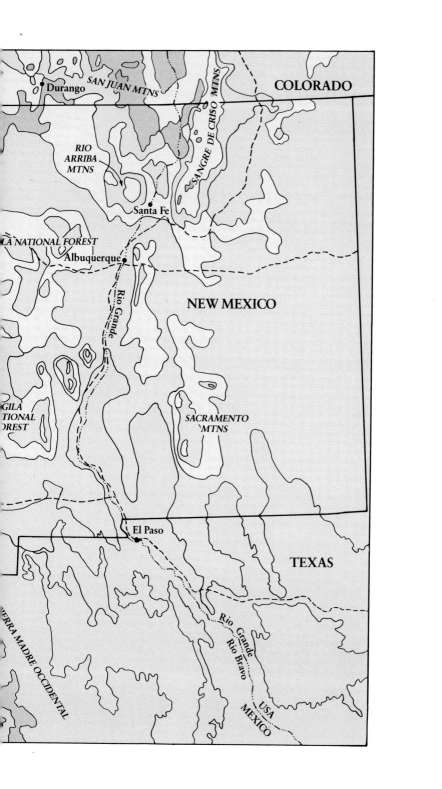

Chaparral Desert scrublands of Arizona and New Mexico are not well known. Only the most distinctive and frequently encountered fungi are listed in this book.

Characteristics of Fungi and Lichens

Fungi are frequently considered to be members of a "third world" of organisms. The features of their feeding bodies that set them so uniquely apart from the plant kingdom, of which they were erroneously considered at one time to be a part, are special adaptations to chemically decompose the tissues of other organisms, particularly plants. They accomplish this through the action of externally secreted enzymes, and thereby obtain their nutrition by nonphotosynthetic means. The feeding bodies of different fungal groups are very similar. A mass of microscopic, branching, thread-like filaments called *hyphae* grow and permeate plant tissue, binding themselves to the fragments that they chemically decompose. The growth promoting nutrients are absorbed through the hyphal walls by an osmotic process. An entire mass of hyphae is called a *mycelium*. It is visible to the unaided eye as a white or colored mat on plant debris or as cablelike strands called *rhizomorphs*. The rhizomorphs often lead underground to a tissue specialized for reproduction, the *primordium*. The primordium, when provided with favorable temperature and moisture, develops into a fruiting body. Mushrooms, macroscopic fruiting bodies, contain microscopic reproductive units, *spores*. Spores function much in the same manner as seeds of flowering plants. They germinate (i.e., grow) following dispersal by wind, water, and animals and produce a new fungus mycelium when deposited in a favorable nutrient environment.

Fungi derive their nutrition from plants in three major ways: as *saprophytes* feeding on dead plant tissue; as *parasites*, feeding on a living host; and as *mutualistic symbionts*, feeding on a living host while at the same time providing some benefit to the host. Nearly every species of vascular plant has at least one species of fungus symbiotically associated with its roots as mycorrhiza. An additional and very common symbiosis of a similar nature is a lichen, the combination of a fungus mycelium that encompasses and feeds on photosynthetic algae. Lichens are a conspicuous component of the mycoflora in all life zones of the Southwest. Their unusual growth forms quickly spark interest and curiosity. A few common lichens representing typical growth forms are described and illustrated.

Some flowering plants derive their nutrition as saprophytes and parasites on mycorrhizal roots, the mycelium of fungi, or on plant matter. They are sometimes mistaken for fungi because in early development, their non-green floral stalks resemble some types of mushrooms.

The mycelium of fungi is rarely found in a form available to collect for eating. This is also true of the reproductive bodies of aquatic fungi and terrestrial *molds*. In contrast, the macroscopic mushrooms of the *sac fungi* (Ascomycetes) and *club fungi* (Basidiomycetes) are avidly sought by *mycophagists*, those who eat fungi. Because the majority of these fungi are host associated, we can use the plants and the life zones of the plants to predict their presence. We can also predict the location of fungi based on their method of feeding on plants. Fruiting bodies of saprophytic fungi will be found on dead plant tissues (roots, stems, and leaves), and parasitic fungi will be in similar positions on living hosts. Mycorrhizal fungi form mushrooms in the vicinity of the root systems to which they are attached, either on or buried beneath the forest floor. Positional relationships are useful criteria in fungal identification.

The naming and subsequent classification of mushroom species are based on characteristics of the fruiting body and the spores. Ascomycetes are called sac fungi because the spores are produced within tiny sacs called *asci*. Basidiomycetes, the club fungi, produce spores on the surfaces of microscopic, club-shaped cells called *basidia*. As you can see, the scientific terminology can aid in both the description and the identification of mushrooms. The most critical difficulty in the correct identification of fungi is the great importance of microscopic characters. Fortunately, the overall shape, texture, color, and sometimes odor and taste of fruiting bodies combined with spore characteristics of the *spore print* serve to separate genera and species of the two groups in most instances.

A third group of fungi found in the Southwest has little resemblance to the other two. The *slime molds*, or Myxomycetes, have a feeding body called a *plasmodium*, with an unwalled mass of cytoplasm instead of hyphae. After a short feeding period, the plasmodium transforms its entire mass into a fruiting body containing spores. These fruiting bodies are often overlooked because of their small size. They are extremely common following rainy periods on the surfaces of plant debris and on the forest floor.

The rapid appearance of mushrooms following warm, moist periods favorable for growth also signifies their rapid demise. Conversely, slower development results in greater longevity. The most ephemeral (short-lived) mushrooms are fleshy. They constitute the majority of edible species. Their edible qualities are diminished by extremes of temperature and moisture. Therefore, fruiting bodies improperly cared for will deteriorate rapidly. Tissues that are tough, leathery, or woody allow the mushroom to persist for several weeks and even years. Perennial fruiting bodies are not generally edible even though they are rarely toxic. In many fleshy mushrooms a special tissue serves to protect the fruiting body as it develops. Called a *peridium* in puffballs and truffles, and a *veil*, present in some pored and gilled mushrooms, this tissue serves as an important identification characteristic. Drought serves to arrest mushroom development. Moisture-starved mushrooms are often smaller than normal. Because mushroom size is often used as descriptive information, care must be taken to observe the conditions under which the fruiting bodies have developed.

Edible and Poisonous Fungi

Most fungus species are eaten by insects or small animals. Edibility for human consumption on the other hand is not known for the majority of species. The pleasure of eating mushrooms comes primarily from the flavors they impart as condiments in cooking. Because fungi are difficult to digest well, we should eat them less to satisfy our hunger than to please our palates. The quantity and variety of wild mushrooms consumed by the public has dramatically increased in recent years. New approaches in mushroom culture have enriched the selection of species offered in the food markets. The number of poisonous mushroom species is relatively small but a very real danger waits for the careless mycophagist. However, with the proper information at hand, most of the deadly poisonous fungi can be readily distinguished from edible species. Those which are difficult to identify are often small, drab colored, nondescript fungi that are not worth a second glance by the discriminating gourmet. If, on the other hand, the challenge sought is identification, there can be no worthier subjects than these.

Mycologists cannot provide unqualified assurance that any species listed as edible is actually edible. Whereas a majority of people experience no adverse effects, individual reaction to mushroom consumption is highly variable and sometimes unpredictable. After an edible species has been identified with certainty, you should proceed with caution on your first try at eating it. Mushroom experts recommend beginning with a small, cooked portion, no more than a quarter cup for adults and a tablespoon or less for children. Notes on edibility have been included in the description of south-western species. **Neither the author nor the publisher accepts responsibility for the reader's identifications or the consequences of eating any of the fungi listed in this book.** For the readers interested in poisonous and hallucinogenic fungi, I highly recommend the books by Lincoff and Mitchell (1977) and Ammirati, Traquir, and Horgen (1985).

Life Zones of the Southwest

In the Southwest, plant communities appear in distinctive zones with more or less discrete boundaries between them. C. Hart Merriam, pioneer naturalist and explorer, defined these ecological distributions as life zones. The zones, diagrammatically illustrated in Figure 2, are related to combinations of temperature and precipitation associated with different elevation (altitude) and latitude. Ascending the mountains of the Southwest is like traveling north. The biotic communities change in a sequence from low-elevation sites that have plant species typical of the southern-latitude deserts to high-elevation sites comprised of plants typically found in the northern latitude forests and tundra. The basis for this relationship, simply stated, is: "There is a temperature decrease of about one degree Fahrenheit (1°F) for each degree of latitude going north and a corresponding decrease of about 1°F for each 250–330 feet of elevation." Annual precipitation increases on mountain slopes at the rate of 4 to 5 inches for every one thousand feet of increased elevation. Therefore, the biotic community responds to the maximum of one factor coincident with the minimum of the other. Temperature generally controls the plant community composition at high elevations and latitude while moisture is the controlling factor at lower elevations and latitudes. Because of lower temperatures and correspondingly higher moisture levels, plant community boundary zones on the more shaded north-facing slopes are always lower in elevation than those on south-facing slopes. Since rainfall and temperature are major determining factors for mushroom productivity, north slopes yield greater mushroom bounty. This bit of information can mean the difference between the success or failure of a mushroom outing.

A successful mushroom hunter needs to know when as well as where a particular fungus fruiting body can be found. Mushrooms are formed seasonally in response to warm temperatures and periods of favorable precipitation. There is also a predictable seasonal fruiting response for

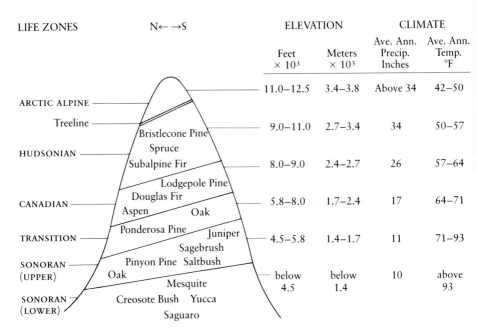

LIFE ZONES	N← →S	ELEVATION		CLIMATE	
		Feet × 10³	Meters × 10³	Ave. Ann. Precip. Inches	Ave. Ann. Temp. °F
		11.0–12.5	3.4–3.8	Above 34	42–50
ARCTIC ALPINE					
Treeline	Bristlecone Pine	9.0–11.0	2.7–3.4	34	50–57
HUDSONIAN	Spruce Subalpine Fir	8.0–9.0	2.4–2.7	26	57–64
	Lodgepole Pine Douglas Fir				
CANADIAN	Aspen Oak	5.8–8.0	1.7–2.4	17	64–71
TRANSITION	Ponderosa Pine Juniper Sagebrush	4.5–5.8	1.4–1.7	11	71–93
SONORAN (UPPER)	Pinyon Pine Saltbush Oak Mesquite	below 4.5	below 1.4	10	above 93
SONORAN (LOWER)	Creosote Bush Yucca Saguaro				

Figure 2. Life Zones of the Southwest

various fungus species. For example, the highly prized morel, *Morchella esculenta*, fruits only in the spring. It appears in the mountain valleys following spring rain and snowmelt, usually in the warm days of late April and early May. But due to the warming in the Sonoran Desert, this same species appears much earlier, in mid to late February if suitable moisture has been received. The Southwest climatic pattern is characteristically a winter precipitation—spring drought, summer precipitation—late-fall drought cycle. The spring and fall droughts are so severe that they promote the desert conditions at low elevations. Welcome relief from heat and drought occurs when moist tropical air from the Gulf of California and Gulf of Mexico passes over the hot landforms and develops intense thundershowers known as the "summer monsoons." This beneficial moisture is particularly heavy in the southern mountains of Arizona and New Mexico at elevations above five thousand feet. Winter precipitation is most often associated with cold, moist air masses from the Pacific Northwest and West. Although the monsoon season is unequivocally the most favorable period for major mushroom fruiting, the general unpredictability of precipitation adequate to stimulate a fungus fruiting response is a source of periodic frustration to the mushroom hunter. Patience is inevitably rewarded because the mushroom production that eventually occurs can exceed one's wildest expectations.

Perennial plants characterize the vegetation of the life zones, and they are good indicators of the prevailing climate, soil factors, and biotic interactions. Because most of the mushroom and truffle species are found in association with conifer forests, forested areas of the Southwest have been outlined on the map (see page 14). The majority of fungi included in this guide represent the typical mycoflora found in four of the five southwestern life zones (biotic communities): Hudsonian (Subalpine), Canadian (Upper Montane), Transition (Lower Montane), and Sonoran (Upper and Lower Sonoran). Brown (1982) has compiled an excellent, comprehensive treatment of the biotic communities of the Southwest to which the reader may refer for additional information. The Arctic–Alpine zone (Tundra) is always above timberline (a region without trees), an area with such severe environmental conditions that mushroom production is greatly limited. Those mushrooms that do occur are often characterized as "snowbank" mushrooms, which are tolerant of cold and obtain moisture from snowmelt.

Trees that appear in the Hudsonian zone include bristlecone pine (*Pinus aristata*), englemann spruce (*Picea englemanni*), and subalpine fir (*Abies lasiocarpa*). Aspen (*Populus tremuloides*) can be found mixed with these conifers or in pure stands in wetter sites. The Canadian zone is characterized by Douglas fir (*Pseudotsuga menzesii*), white fir (*Abies concolor*), limber pine (*Pinus flexilis*), englemann spruce, blue spruce, and aspen. Ponderosa pine (*Pinus ponderosa*) dominates the Transition zone, along with a limited mixture of gambel oak (*Quercus gambelii*), manzanita (*Arctostaphylos* spp.), and buckbrush (*Ceanothus integerrimus*). In the northern mountains, lodgepole pine (*Pinus contorta*) is mixed with or replaces ponderosa pine as the dominant tree species with snowberry (*Symphoricarpos* spp.) and huckleberry or whortleberry (*Vaccinium* spp.) in the understory. Below the Transition zone, a foothills woodland composed of pinyon pine (*Pinus edulis*), juniper (*Juniperus* spp.), and evergreen oaks (*Quercus* spp.) constitutes the Upper Sonoran zone. Sagebrush (*Artemisia* spp.) is often found in the understory of this woodland and in adjacent areas.

The composition of the Lower Sonoran is variable according to precipitation patterns and elevation. In most of the Southwest there is a widespread desert scrubland below the pinyon-juniper woodland, often with an intervening semidesert grassland. These desert lands—the Great Basin, Mohave, Chihuahuan, and Sonoran—are characterized by low-growing, widely spaced shrubs dominated by creosote bush (*Larrea tridentata*), shadscale (*Atriplex* spp.), sagebrush (*Artemisia* spp.), mesquite (*Prosopis* spp.), paloverde (*Cercidium* spp.), and various species of cacti.

Transcending the boundaries of the various zones is the Riparian zone. It is characterized by winter deciduous hardwood trees and shrubs that occupy temporary and permanent drainages of rivers and streams. The most prevalent tree species are alder (*Alnus* spp.), ash (*Fraxinus*), box elder (*Acer negundo*), cottonwood (*Populus* spp.), locust (*Robinia* spp.), salt cedar (*Tamarisk chinensis*), oak (*Quercus* spp.), walnut (*Juglans* sp.), and willow (*Salix* spp.). In areas with moderate precipitation, stands of oak extend beyond the immediate Riparian zone and constitute a popular and productive woodland for mushroom collecting. Most of the streams of the Southwest have intermittent stream flows with variable discharge volume. Mushroom production is generally unpredictable, making the Riparian zone unpredictable for collecting and one of the least studied for associated fungi. Because of the diversity of higher plants, it may have a wealth of undiscovered and unrecorded mushrooms, a potential gold mine for the mushroom enthusiast who has time and patience to spare.

Collection and Identification of Fungi

COLLECTION SUGGESTIONS

Problems in the collection and identification of fungi are inevitable. Every serious mushroom hunter should consult more than one text to assure proper identification. The "do's" and "don'ts" of mushroom collecting are treated in detail by authors of other mushroom guides cross-referenced in this book. I consider the following points most essential:

A. Collect the entire fruiting body, several of them if possible in different stages of development. If there is some doubt as to whether individual collections are the same, wrap them separately in containers, preferably in waxed-paper bags or sheets, twisted at the ends to seal in moisture. Paper bags make suitable containers but plastic bags do not. They invariably cause fleshy fungi to decompose more rapidly.

B. Immediately label the collection with an identification name or number that refers to a field description of the specimen you have recorded in a field notebook. Field records should include: date of collection; location; habitat characteristics to include identity of the plant host and/or vegetation in the immediate vicinity; and the position of the fruiting body (whether it is on the ground, on plant debris, attached to plant surfaces, and growing separately or in clusters of separate or attached fruiting bodies). Most importantly, notes should be taken on essential identification characteristics of the fruiting body that will change with time and transport. These characteristics include: surface colors, bruising reaction, odor, texture (i.e., slimy, *viscid*, mealy, dry or wet), and evidence of exuded droplets or *latex*. Taste is a useful character but the small amount chewed and applied to the tongue should *never* be swallowed. The color reaction of the tissues to an application of a 5 percent solution of potassium hydroxide is particularly important in the identification of truffles and false truffles.

C. Always make a spore print for the fruiting bodies that have exposed fertile surfaces. To obtain a spore print, place the surfaces of the spore-bearing tissue face down on a sheet of white paper. Unless the fruiting body is immature, spores will be deposited on the paper after several hours, revealing their characteristic color in mass. Spore prints are particularly necessary in the identification of fleshy, gilled, and pored mushrooms. Other key characters of these fungi that you will be asked to evaluate include: presence and condition of the veils; attachment characteristics of the *gills* to the *stalk*; presence of a cup at the base of the stalk, and variations in the stalk diameter and length.

D. Remove as much extraneous debris from the fruiting body surface as possible. You may wish to look for the presence of fungus-fly larvae in the tissues since their presence leads to fruiting body deterioration. It is not a good idea to eat fungi damaged by insects or those partially decayed by bacteria and molds.

E. A hand lens and a plastic ruler are helpful in making essential in-field measurements of the fruiting body. In some cases it is not possible to identify a collection to species without observing the microscopic characteristics of the spores and the cellular details of the fruiting body. In situations where you intend to consume the fungus, you should not rely on an "educated guess," but should refer the specimen to someone who can make the necessary microscopic examination.

FUNGUS CLASSIFICATION

The common name for a species is useful, but it is not uniformly applied or accepted in many cases. The scientific name on the other hand is universally accepted. It is a Latin binomial (two names): the first is used to designate the genus, a group of closely related species, and the second designates species, a group of individuals that share similar reproductive characteristics. Because sexual compatibility has not been worked out for many of the fungi, we must rely upon characteristics of the fruiting body to separate species. The binomial is always italicized in published works and the generic name is always capitalized. Occasionally alternative names for the species exist as synonyms. Usually these names are no longer scientifically correct but remain in common usage. In this guide, the synonyms are given to aid in updating earlier literature. The name of the mycologist(s) who first described and named the species is listed (in an abbreviated form) after the species name. If the name of the fungus was transferred to another genus, the author of the change is listed after the original author's name and the original author's name is then placed in parentheses. Such a change can be illustrated for the common "Shaggy Mane" mushroom:

Coprinus comatus   (Mull. ex Fr.)   S. F. Gray.
genus   species   original author   author of change

Groups of related genera are classified as families, and related families are placed in orders. To assist in the recognition of these classification levels, the suffix "*-ales*" is added to ordinal names and the suffix "*-aceae*" to family names. Groups of orders are placed in classes and the class suffix is "*-mycetes.*" Quite frequently the latinized names of classes, orders, and families are employed as common names. For example, slime molds are occasionally referred to as "Myxomycetes" even though there are more classes of slime molds than just the Myxomycetes. Likewise the "sac fungi" are referred to as "Ascomycetes" and the "club fungi" are referred to as "Basidiomycetes."

It is not always possible to determine with the unaided eye whether an unknown collection possesses asci or basidia and therefore whether it is a club or sac fungus. However, there are distinctive, macroscopic characteristics, such as shape and texture of the fruiting body, that can be used to accurately place unknowns in their proper group. Two types of keys are provided to assist the reader in identifying an unknown collection. The first is a key that simply illustrates the characteristic growth form of fourteen major fungus groups and the lichens. The descriptive terms that accompany the names of these groups are used in the second key, which is a narrative key. Both keys direct the reader to the page where each group is individually described and discussed.

HOW TO USE THE KEYS

Narrative keys are used as an outline to the distinctive characteristics of an unknown specimen belonging to several fungus groups. A series of keys are provided starting with the one describing the largest groups of fungi and fungus relatives (as in classes) followed by keys leading to progressively smaller groups (as in orders, then families, and finally genus and species).

The characteristics are presented in contrasting pairs or couplets, thus allowing you to choose those features that fit your observations of the specimen and to eliminate others. After making a series of choices, you will come to a final pair of couplets. One of these will complete all of the characteristics you have selected and will provide the name of the group to which your specimen belongs.

Let us assume that you have a specimen in hand whose appearance closely resembles the illustration of a chanterelle in the Picture Key on page 29. On this basis you may proceed directly to the description of the chanterelles on page 122, or you may use the Narrative Key to the Major Groups of Fungi on page 36. Using this key you will make a series of choices that will lead you to couplet seven. Because your specimen is fleshy with a cap and gills attached to a stalk, you choose couplet eight. The gills have knifelike edges and you are directed to the key describing the Agaricales, eliminating the chanterelles as a choice. The presence of gills eliminates the family Boletaceae in the first couplet of this key. Because the gills are light-colored you may assume the spore print will be white and proceed to couplet three. (It is best to verify spore print color until you gain experience with a wide variety of gilled mushrooms.) Since the gills do not leave a waxy substance when rubbed between your fingers, you are directed to couplet six. The flesh of your specimen does not crumble when squeezed so you are further directed to the species described in the family Tricholomataceae on page 80.

Upon reading the description of the genera and species representative of the family, you will discover the false chanterelle *Hygrophoriopsis aurantiaca*, described as a look-alike for the chanterelle, *Cantharellus cibarius*, matching it in general shape, size, and color. However, the gill characteristics and odor of your specimen clearly match it with the description of the false chanterelle. A photograph supplements the species narrative and assists in conveying to you those characteristics that are difficult to put into words. The species description includes information on fruiting body and spore characteristics, as well as comments regarding related species, life zone and habitat, seasonal occurrence, and edibility. Cross-references are provided allowing you to make fuller comparisons to substantiate your identification.

CROSS-REFERENCES

A unique feature of this book is the inclusion of a cross-reference system to assist in species identification. The references listed below are all available in bookstores and libraries, and all but the How-to-Know guides by Smith and by Hale contain helpful, color photographs. In the species descriptions that follow, the cross-reference codes are enclosed in parentheses.

Code	*Reference*
AMD	Arora, D. 1986. *Mushrooms Demystified*. 2nd Ed. Ten Speed Press, Berkeley.
BSM	Bessett, A., and W. J. Sundberg. 1987. *Mushrooms, A Quick Reference Guide to Mushrooms of North America*. Macmillan Field Guides. Macmillan Pub. Co., New York.
HKL	Hale, M. E. 1979. *How to Know the Lichens*. 2nd Ed. The Pictured Key Nature Series. Wm. C. Brown Co. Pub., Dubuque, Iowa.
LAS	Lincoff, G. H. 1981. *The Audubon Society Field Guide to North American Mushrooms*. A.A. Knopf, Inc., New York.
MNA	Miller, O. K. 1977. *Mushrooms of North America*. E. P. Dutton & Co., Dubuque, Iowa.
MSM	McKenney, Margaret, and Daniel E. Stuntz. 1987. *The New Savory Wild Mushroom*. Revised and Enlarged by Joseph Ammirati. University of Washington Press, Seattle.
SWM	Smith, A. H. 1975. *A Field Guide to the Western Mushrooms*. University of Michigan Press, Ann Arbor.
SGM	Smith, A. H., H. V. Smith, and Nancy S. Weber. 1979. *How to Know the Gilled Mushrooms*. The Pictured Key Nature Series. Wm. C. Brown Co. Pub., Dubuque, Iowa.
SNGM	Smith, A. H., H. V. Smith, N. S. Weber. 1973. *How to Know the Non-Gilled Mushrooms*. 2nd Ed. The Pictured Key Nature Series. Wm. C. Brown. Co. Pub., Dubuque, Iowa.

Picture Key to the Major Groups
of Fungi and Fungus Relatives

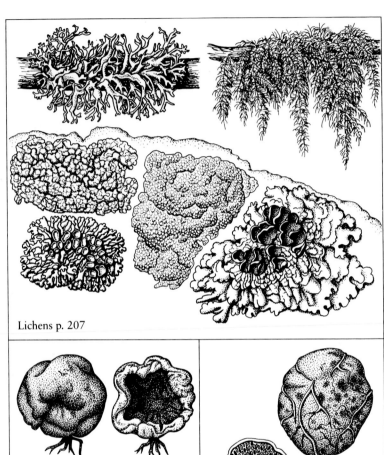

Lichens p. 207

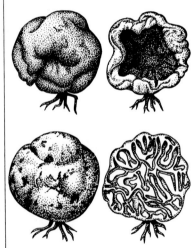

Tuberlike Ascomycetes p. 186
(Truffles)

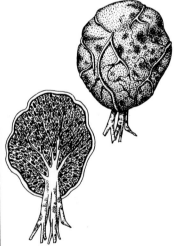

Tuberlike Basidiomycetes p. 186
(False Truffles)

Cantharellaceae p. 121 (Chanterelles)

Agaricales p. 42 (Fleshy Gilled Mushrooms)

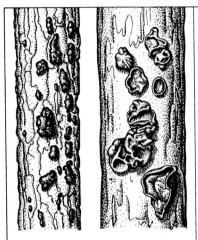

Tremellales & Auriculariales p. 142
(Jelly Fungi)

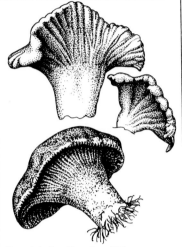

Parasitic Sac Fungi p. 171

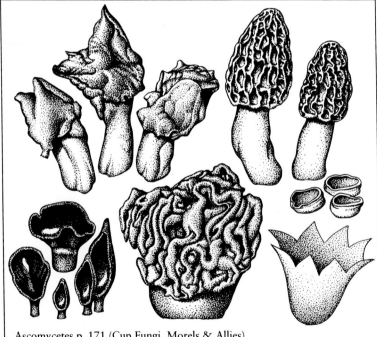

Ascomycetes p. 171 (Cup Fungi, Morels & Allies)

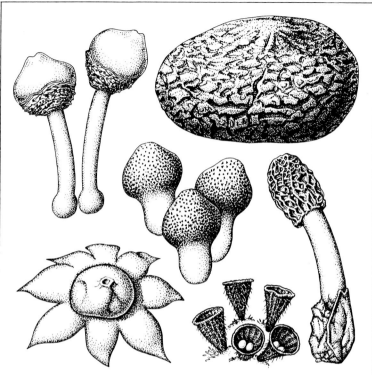

Gasteromycetes p. 146 (Puffballs & Allies)

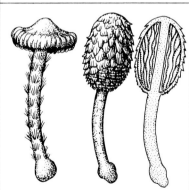

Agaricoid Gasteromycetes p. 146
(Stomach Fungi)

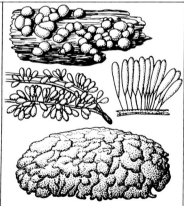

Myxomycetes p. 204 (Slime Molds)

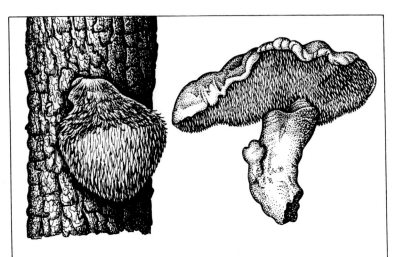

Spinose Aphyllophorales p. 121 (Teeth Fungi)

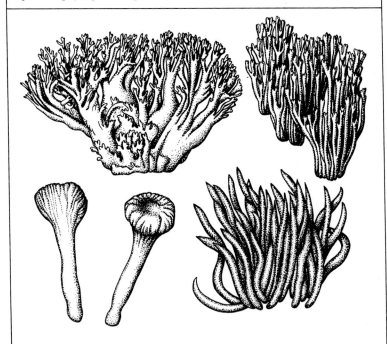

Coralloid Aphyllophorales p. 121 (Coral Fungi)

Poroid Aphyllophorales p. 121 (Polypores)

Boletaceae p. 42 (Fleshy, Pored Mushrooms)

Narrative Key to the Major Groups of Fungi and Fungus Relatives

1a. Fruiting bodies when present as small colored discs or minute dark bumps on a flattened or erect thallus; thallus leafy or bushy with a dry, leathery texture, attached to the surfaces of rocks and trees . . . . (p. 207) Lichens

1b. Not as above 2

    2a. Fruiting body subterranean (hypogeous) and potatolike (tuberous) in form; spore mass (*gleba*) retained inside a protective case (peridium) at maturity 3

    2b. Fruiting body above ground (*epigeous*) 4

3a. Young fruiting body fleshy and brittle when sectioned; gleba as convoluted folds of fertile tissue: solid and marbled or with several hollow cavities . . . . . . (p. 186) Tuberlike Ascomycetes (truffles)

3b. Young fruiting body firm or *cartilaginous* when sectioned; gleba with poroid chambers which gelatinize in some species at maturity . . . . (p. 186) Tuberlike Basidiomycetes (false truffles)

    4a. Fruiting body of one of the following types: (1) resembling balls of various shapes, white when young; peridium encasing a powdery gleba; in some the outer peridium splitting to form basal starlike rays; (2) resembling a small funnel-shaped cup containing miniature egglike structures (*peridioles*); (3) stalk present and distinct from an apical spore case; or (4) arising from a hypogeous primordium as a variously shaped stalk; the gleba exposed or enclosed releasing a foul-smelling odor at maturity . . . . (p. 146) Gasteromycetes (puffballs and allies)

    4b. Not as above 5

5a. Mature fruiting body resembling a stalked, gilled mushroom but the peridial tissue and attachment of gill plates preventing the discharge of spores . . . . (p. 146) Agaricoid Gasteromycetes

5b. Not as above 6

    6a. Fruiting bodies resembling miniature puffballs without or with minute stalks, produced from a slime body (plasmodium); the spore mass powdery and readily released from a fragile peridium . . (p. 204) Myxomycetes (slime molds)

    6b. Not as above 7

7a. Fruiting bodies fleshy, consisting of a cap (*pileus*) with gills, occasionally tough but soon decaying; stalk present or absent 8

7b. Not as above 9

    8a. Gills as wrinkled veins, folds or blunt edged plates, extending from an uneven cap margin downward along the stalk, fruit body usually vase- or trumpet-shaped . . . . . .
    . . . . (p. 121) Cantharellaceae (Chanterelles)

    8b. Gills tapered to knifelike edges, variously attached or free from the stalk; stalk present or absent . . . .
    . . . . (p. 42) Agaricales (fleshy mushrooms)

9a. Fruiting body consisting of a cap with a layer of vertically oriented tubes opening by pores on the lower surface; or undersurface of cap smooth; stalk present or absent; gills when present tough and leathery 10

9b. Not as above 11

    10a. Cap tough and woody, often perennial; stalk present or absent, often laterally attached when present . . . .
    . . . . (p. 121) Poroid Aphyllophorales (polypores)

    10b. Cap fleshy, tissues readily decaying, stalk more or less centrally attached (p. 42) Boletaceae (fleshy, pored mushrooms)

11a. Fruiting body one of the following: (1) fleshy or tough and woody bearing erect or pendant spines; stalk present or absent; (2) resembling certain kinds of coral with a multibranched structure, the branches flattened; in some as single, club-shaped stalks; or (3) bracketlike or as resupinate crusts with smooth spore bearing surfaces 12

11b. Not as above 14

    12a. Fruiting bodies coralloid, club-shaped or with toothlike spines 13

12b. Fruiting bodies bracket or crustlike with smooth spore
  bearing surfaces . . . . . (p. 121) Crustose Aphyllophorales
  (crust fungi)

13a. Fruiting bodies with toothlike spines . . . . (p. 121) Spinose
  Aphyllophorales   (teeth fungi)

13b. Fruiting bodies coralloid or club-shaped . . . .
  . . . . (p. 121) Coralloid Aphyllophorales (coral fungi)

  14a. Fruiting body jellylike, in some soft cartilaginous, shaped
    like shallow cups or raised amorphous masses (one species
    tongue-shaped with gelatinous spines . . . .
    . . . . . (p. 142) Tremellales and Auriculariales (jelly fungi)

  14b. Not as above 15

15a. Fruiting body one of the following types: (1) cup-, saucer-, or
  funnel-shaped, the flesh firm and sometimes brittle; (2) caps
  sponge-, lobed-, or saddle-shaped; stalk present; odor often fragrant . . . . (p. 171) Ascomycetes (cup fungi, morels and allies)

15b. Fruiting bodies somewhat mushroom-shaped, the surface a minutely bumpy mat colored red-orange or green . . . .
  . . . . (p. 171) parasitic sac fungi

Mushrooms and Truffles of the Southwest

Club Fungi

The great diversity of fruiting body forms provides a convenient means for the identification of Basidiomycetes. Most of the members of the order Aphyllophorales are tough to woody and can be separated from one another based on the type of *hymenophore*, the structure bearing the fertile layer (*hymenium*) of basidia and basidiospores on its exposed surface. The basidiospores are forcefully discharged at maturity. The fleshy to leathery upright branches of the coral fungi distinguish them from the teeth fungi with spinelike hymenophores, the pore fungi with tubular hymenophores and the crust fungi which lack a differentiated hymenophore. Most of the fleshy fungi with a fertile layer formed on the exposed surfaces of gill-like ridges (*chanterelles*), tubes (*boletes*), or gills (*agarics*) all have a caplike pileus either supported by a stalk or attached more or less directly to the substratum. These mushroom types, in turn, are quite different from the "stomach" fungi that produce a fertile tissue, the *gleba*, inside a fleshy to papery spore case, the peridium. The stomach fungi belong to the class Gasteromycetes in which the general form and tissue arrangement of the gleba are distinctive for each particular group. The spores of the Gasteromycetes are not forcibly discharged at maturity. The puffballs have a papery saclike peridium enclosing a powdery spore mass and in many species the spores are released from an apical pore. Some Gasteromycetes are stalked with apically positioned spore sacs or have hornlike stalks inside of which are produced wet, foul-smelling spore masses. Those that have experienced the odor of the stinkhorns have no difficulty in their identification. Those Gasteromycetes that have a gill-like gleba are referred to as Agaricoid Gasteromycetes. The hypogeous, tuberlike forms of the Gasteromycetes are called false truffles. A great variety of false truffle species exists, most of which are mycorrhizal associates of coniferous trees.

FLESHY GILLED AND FLESHY PORED FUNGI: ORDER AGARICALES

The fleshy fungi included in this group are those most commonly referred to as mushrooms. They are called "boletes" if the fertile tissue is arranged as a series of descending tubes with lower ends open to form a field of pores. The boletes are treated either in the family Boletaceae or in a separate order, the Boletales. The remaining families constitute an extremely diverse group of gilled mushrooms called "agarics."

The families of agarics and their inclusive genera are most easily distinguished from one another on the basis of spore color, the architecture of the gills (especially the manner in which they are attached to the stalk), and the presence and condition of veils left as remnants of the primordium. The universal veil appears as a cup (*volva*) at the base of the stalk and the partial veil forms a distinct ring, the *annulus,* a line of tissue remnants which encircle the stalk. Ease of separation of the cap from the stalk is also an important feature. In most cases where the stalk can be separated from the cap, the gills are not attached to the cap.

In the key to the families of the Agaricales, the reader is directed to pages where the genera contained in the family are described. Because the treatment of the species within each genus is selective, no key to them is provided and they are presented in alphabetical order. The description in combination with photo illustration and cross-references will assist in making positive identifications of unknowns. The cross-references provide more comprehensive species descriptions that include microscopic characteristics, and in most cases additional color illustrations.

Key to the Major Families of the Agaricales

1a. Cap with tubes, the lower surface poroid . . . . . (p. 44) Boletaceae
1b. Cap with gills, the lower surface lamellate 2
    2a. Spore print white or light yellow 3
        (light green in the case of *Chlorophyllum*, p. 62)
    2b. Not as above 7
3a. Gills free; cap easily separating from the stalk; flesh distinct from the stalk; ring on the stalk present or absent 4
3b. Not as above 5

4a. Fruiting body with veil remnants as a cup (volva) at the base of the stalk and loose tissue on the cap surface and present or absent as a ring (annulus) on the stalk; cap usually slimy to viscid when moist . . . . (p. 54) Amanitaceae

4b. Fruiting body without a volva; annulus present; cap dry and often scaly . . . . (p. 60) Lepiotaceae

5a. Gills thick, waxy in texture and widely spaced, attached to and often descending the stalk; cap often brightly colored . . . . (p. 64) Hygrophoraceae

5b. Gills not waxy 6

6a. Flesh of fruiting body brittle and crumbly when crushed; cut gills producing a clear to colored latex (in *Lactarius*); fruiting bodies generally robust . . . . . (p. 68) Russulaceae

6b. Not as above in all respects . . . (p. 80) Tricholomataceae

7a. Spore print black, purplish gray, gray-olive, or gray (not brown); gills either free and liquefying in age or *decurrent* on stalk and persistent 8

7b. Spore print not as above 9

8a. Gills free, disintegrating as an inky black fluid in age (*Coprinus*) or intact and black to dark brown . . . . (p. 101) Coprinaceae

8b. Gills attached, descending the stalk . . . . (p. 104) Gomphidiaceae

9a. Spore print dark purplish brown, light brown, or chocolate brown; membranous veil remnants usually present 10

9b. Not as above 11

10a. Gills free, white or pink when young, turning chocolate brown; fruiting body mostly fleshy; veil usually present as an annulus . . . . (p. 107) Agaricaceae

10b. Gills attached to stalk; fruiting body firm to fibrous; spore print brown to purple-black; veil usually present but not often as an annulus . . . . (p. 110) Strophariaceae

11a. Spore print reddish brown, cinnamon-brown to orange rusty brown; often with a cobweblike veil (*cortina*) attached to the stalk and cap when young or veil membranous   (p. 112) Cortinariaceae

11b. Spore print dull pink to brick red or salmon; spores angular (in Entolomataceae) . . . . (p. 120) Pluteaceae (Volvariaceae) and Entolomataceae (Rhodophyllaceae)

Family Boletaceae

Many of the best, edible fungi can be found in this group of pored, fleshy mushrooms. They are abundant in the Southwest and many species are mycorrhizal with both coniferous and deciduous trees. The species included here are so diverse that some authors consider the family as an order, entirely separate from the Agaricales. Major characteristics for identification of genera include: texture of the cap; color, shape, and arrangement of the pores; stalk ornamentations as *scabers* or as *glandular dots*; color of the spore deposit; color reaction on bruising; and presence or absence of veil tissue. The majority of the southwestern boletes can be assigned to three major genera. Nearly all species of *Suillus* are associated with conifers. Their fruiting bodies are characterized by narrow to elongated, angular tubes variously colored in shades of yellow or yellow-orange and arranged along the radii of the cap. Some species have dry caps with veil tissue at the margin or on the stalk and the stalk is not ornamented. Those with viscid or sticky caps usually lack veil tissue and the stalks are ornamented with conspicuous glandular dots. *Leccinum* has dry stalks with conspicuous roughenings or scabers that darken with age. The caps rarely possess yellow coloration and veil tissue is lacking. The largest genus, *Boletus*, lacks the combination of features found in the other two genera. It can be recognized by its generally robust fruiting body, netlike ridges that often ornament the stalk, its usually dry cap, and the uniform, lower surface of red, yellow or whitish tubes. Species whose tube mouths bruise bluish or are colored in various shades of red may be poisonous. These species and any specimens that are soft and old should not be selected for eating. Species of *Strobilomyces*, *Gyroporus*, and *Tylopilus* have been occasionally collected in the evergreen hardwood forests and the Riparian zone of the Southwest. The collection list is growing as more mushroom hunters explore these plant communities. Boletes typical of eastern North America, especially those with red pigmentation on the tubes and stalk, occur with those typical of the West in southern New Mexico and Arizona. Arora (*AMD*) has constructed a useful key to some of the common species found in this region.

Boletus barrowsii

Boletus barrowsii Thiers & A. H. Smith

Fruiting body large, 6–25 cm broad (similar in appearance to *B. edulis*); cap dry and smooth, pallid to gray when young becoming tan to buff at maturity; stalk concolorous with the cap, sometimes enlarged at the base or more often of equal thickness throughout its length; tube surface off-white to pallid yellow ochraceous; the tubes tinged olivaceous at maturity; spore print dark olive brown. (AMD)

COMMENTS   This large bolete is a species characteristic of the ponderosa pine forest in the Transition zone and is unique to the Southwest. Unlike *B. edulis* it is rarely found in higher elevation forests. Both species have been found growing together in association with ponderosa pine and both are equally edible and choice. It is one of the most frequently collected table mushrooms in the region.

Boletus chrysenteron Fr.

Caps 3–8 cm broad, olive brown to dark brown with a velvety, dry surface that separates into a network of cracks exposing whitish to yellow tissue

Boletus chrysenteron

Boletus edulis

below; the exposed tissue turns pinkish red near the cracks; tubes bright yellow becoming yellow brown to olive brown at maturity; quickly staining greenish blue on bruising; stalk reddish over yellow flesh beneath, the pigmentation strongest at midpoint toward the base. (AMD, LAS, MNA, MSM)

COMMENTS   Also known as *Xerocomus chrysenteron* it is similar in appearance to *B. zelleri* which has not been reported from the Southwest. (AMD, LAS, MSM) It is widely distributed in mixed deciduous conifer forests, especially in the Canadian and Riparian zones. Some consider it edible but it is definitely not choice.

Boletus edulis Bull. ex. Fr.

Fruiting body large and robust with a reddish brown, broadly convex cap up to 30 cm broad, the surface uneven and slightly polished, sticky and slippery when wet; tubes white when young turning yellowish to drab olive brown in age, pored surface noticeably sunken near the site of stalk attachment; stalk swollen (*clavate*) at the base tapering to a narrow apex ornamented with white, netlike ridges, the ridges and the stalk surface becoming whitish tan in age; spore print olive brown. (AMD, BSM, LAS, MNA, MSM)

COMMENTS   Called the "King Bolete" or "Cep," this extremely popular edible bolete is found worldwide. It is also a favorite food item for fungus gnats. Their larval stages quickly colonize the fleshy tissues and accelerate decomposition, thus rendering the fruiting body inedible. Diced tissues dehydrated in a food dryer can be stored for long periods of time and reconstituted with water for use as a condiment in cooking. This bolete fruits in the Canadian and Hudsonian zones, sometimes in massive quantities.

Leccinum insigne Smith, Thiers & Watling

Caps reddish orange to orange-brown, 5–18 cm broad, minutely hairy to smooth and polished in age; pore surface white becoming yellowish brown and bruising pallid brown to bluish brown; stalk white ornamented with reddish brown scabers that turn black; tissues when bruised first turn reddish gray and then bluish gray; spore print yellow brown. (AMD, LAS, MNA)

Leccinum insigne

COMMENTS   A common species under aspen and pine in the Canadian and Transition zones, *L. insigne* is reported to be edible and good. In wet sites of the Riparian zone with mixed forest types it can occur in great abundance. A similar species, *L. montanum*, occurs under aspen. Its cap is pale yellowish brown to brown, the stalk ornamentation is very dense at the base, and its flesh does not stain on bruising. *L. aurantiacum* (LAS, MSM) is similar in appearance but is generally more robust and the flesh stains burgundy red immediately after bruising.

Leccinum subalpinum Thiers

Caps 5–25 cm broad, dry and finely (*tomentose*) hairy over the entire surface, rusty red to rich reddish brown, tubes off-white to pallid cream bruising light reddish brown with yellowish green tints, sterile at the cap margin with marginal flaps of veil tissue; stalk broad at the base and narrowed at the apex, copiously covered with dark brown scabers; spore print yellow brown to brown.

Leccinum subalpinum

COMMENTS   This species is found at high elevations in mixed conifer forests particularly spruce-fir in the Hudsonian zone. It fruits in midsummer. Like most Leccinums it is edible.

Suillus americanus (Pk.) Snell

Caps 3–10 cm broad, sticky when wet, yellow to cinnamon buff, streaked with reddish *scales*, a cottony veil attached to the margin; flesh yellow staining brown; stalk 3–9 cm long and up to 1.0 cm thick, yellow and covered with reddish glandular dots, without a ring and nearly equal; tube mouths yellow to yellow brown. (LAS, MNA)

COMMENTS   Both *S. americanus* and *S. sibiricus* are associated with 5-needle pines, the former with pines in eastern North America and the latter in the Pacific Northwest and West. Arora (AMD) speculates that those associated with limber pine and southwestern white pine of the Canadian and Hudsonian zone of the Southwest may represent a hybrid between the two. Both of those in the photo illustration came from the same locality. They

Suillus americanus

Suillus brevipes

Suillus granulatus

are not reported to be a favored edible and in one case an allergic reaction has been noted.

Suillus brevipes (Pk.) Kuntz

Caps 4–10 cm broad, reddish brown to dark brown fading tan to cinnamon, smooth and slimy when moist; flesh white to yellowish, not changing color on bruising; stalk short, 2–7 cm long and up to 3 cm thick, white to light yellow, without glandular dots; ring absent; tubes strong yellow, up to 1 cm deep and slightly decurrent on stalk. (LAS, MSM)
COMMENTS   This species is abundant and widely distributed under conifers, especially 2- and 3-needle pines. It is sometimes confused with the darker forms of *S. granulatus* and with *S. albidipes* which has a roll of cottony veil tissue at the cap margin. It is edible and good if the slimy skin of the cap is removed before cooking.

Suillus granulatus (Fr.) Kuntz

Caps broadly convex, viscid to slimy when wet, pallid yellow when young becoming cinnamon on a pale buff background; tube mouths angular, pale to bright yellow but dingy ocher yellow in age; stalk whitish outside but developing yellowish tints as does the cap tissue, pinkish to reddish cinnamon glandular dots near the cap or covering the entire stalk; spore print is cinnamon. (LAS, MNA, MSM)

COMMENTS   Fruiting bodies are scattered to clustered in pine forests throughout summer and fall following periods of rain. It is a highly variable species with regard to fruiting body coloration and it resembles several other species with which it is associated, including *S. pseudobrevipes* and *S. kaibabensis*. *S. kaibabensis* is virtually indistinguishable from the yellow forms of *S. granulatus*. It is found under ponderosa pine on the Colorado Plateau, particularly when sagebrush is in the understory. *S. pseudobrevipes* has a short stalk with inconspicuous glandular dots, veil tissue at the margin of a yellow to cinnamon brown cap. It is considered edible.

Suillus lakei (Murr.) A. H. Smith & Thiers

Caps broadly convex, with an inrolled margin and covered with reddish to orange buff scales which may disappear in age; tubes are shallow and dingy yellow but rapidly turn brown on bruising; stalk enlarged downward but becoming narrow at the base, cinnamon-colored and brighter yellow below the cap, lacking ornamentation but with a narrow annulus just below the cap, flesh bruising blue; spore print cinnamon brown. (AMD, LAS, MSM, SWM)

COMMENTS   *S. lakei* is found only under Douglas fir in the Canadian zone where it is common and abundant in late summer and early fall. It is edible when young but the quality rapidly deteriorates as it matures.

Suillus sibiricus (Sing) Singer

Cap bright yellow to ocher yellow, 3–10 cm broad, smooth and slimy when moist, ornamented with scattered reddish brown to dark brown scales or streaks; flesh yellow staining somewhat vinaceous when bruised; stalk 3–11 cm long and up to 1.5 cm thick, equal throughout length, yellow to yellow ocher, covered with brown to blackish brown glandular dots; ring present or inconspicuous, tubes mustard yellow to yellow brown in age. (AMD, SWM)

COMMENTS   See *S. americanus*

Suillus lakei

Suillus sibiricus

Suillus tomentosus

Suillus tomentosus Singer, Thiers & Miller

Caps 5–9 cm broad, orange yellow to orange buff, sticky when wet and covered with grayish to medium reddish brown scales or matted *fibrils*; flesh yellow orange to pinkish orange becoming brownish orange in age, staining bluegreen on exposure; tubes pale yellow to dark cinnamon, bluing when cut, angular and up to 1 mm diameter; stalk colored as the cap, glandular dotted; ring absent. (LAS, MSM)

COMMENTS   Fruiting bodies often abundant, scattered in the duff of lodgepole pine and occasionally other conifers. It has not been reported in the mountains of southern Arizona, New Mexico, and Mexico where lodgepole pine is absent. It is considered to be a poor-quality edible.

Family Amanitaceae

Of the many species of Amanita a few are edible and some of the many poisonous varieties are deadly poisonous. These species account for a large percentage of deaths attributed to mushroom poisoning. Several poisonous species resemble the edible ones and therefore the eating of any Amanita is not recommended. Cases of mistaken identity occur most frequently when immature specimens are collected or when some of the major identifying characteristics go unobserved or are missing on the fruiting body.

The essential features of Amanita include: a cottony or membranous cup (volva) at the base of the stalk; a ring of veil tissue (annulus) on the stalk (this tissue is not present in the *Amanitopsis* group and it often falls away in mature *Amanita* species); white gills that are free from the stalk; a white to light yellow spore print; removable membranous patch or patches of veil tissue on the cap (this tissue may be absent in some species). In many species, the cap margin has fine lines or striations which represent the gill attachment showing through the cap tissue from below. The characteristics of the volva are very important in species identifications. In some species the volva is indistinct and other characters must be consulted.

The only other genus of the family, *Limacella*, is not common in the Southwest. However, it is widespread and abundant occasionally in some years in high-elevation coniferous forests. It is readily distinguished from *Amanita* by copious slime on the veil tissue and the absence of a volva. (AMD, LAS, MNA)

Amanita caesarea (Fr.) Schw.

Fruiting body often large and robust; cap brightly colored in youth, peach-red in the center and apricot yellow toward the margin, fading in age to light pinkish-orange at the center and light ochraceous yellow at the margin; 10–18 cm broad when fully expanded, a large piece of white veil tissue often remaining attached near the margin; gills crowded together and broad, light yellow and free from the stalk but slightly attached when young; the stalk thick and up to 20 cm long with a slightly bulbous base; annulus firmly attached to the stalk beneath the cap, light yellow to yellow ocher, pendant, large and membranous; the volva large, extending up one-third the length of the stalk with a free margin that is often split or torn; spore print ochraceous yellow, often visible as a powdery remnant on the annulus surface; spore print light ocher yellow. (AMD, LAS, MNA)

COMMENTS   This spectacular Amanita is found in great abundance in arcs beneath ponderosa pine following heavy summer and early fall rain. It is clearly related to the edible "Caesar's Amanita" of European fame, but it lacks the brilliant orange-red coloration of the cap and differs in several

Amanita caesarea

other microscopic characteristics. The dull orange form of *A. calyptrata* is similar in the possession of a yellow cap but has brown at the center in mature specimens and is found in southern California. (AMD, BSM, MSM) Our southwestern Amanita may well represent a species intermediate between *A. caesarea* and *A. calyptrata*. Both are considered edible and choice species but caution is advised because of the poisonous reputation of the genus.

Amanita gemmata (Fr.) Gill.

Caps 5–10 cm broad, convex in youth becoming flat in age, light yellow to light yellowish buff, sticky when wet, with scattered veil remnants that slide off when the cap pushes through the leaf litter or that wash off in wet weather; margin smooth to radially lined; gills white to pale cream and crowded; stalk slender and up to 20 cm long, with or without a fragile, pendant annulus that falls away in age; volva shallow, short and closely pressed around the swollen stalk base, patchy volval tissue extending a short way up the stalk in some specimens; spore print white. (BSM, LAS, MSM)

Amanita gemmata

COMMENTS This is a difficult Amanita to identify because it often loses its characteristic veil remnants on the cap and stalk, leaving it pallid and nondescript. Although it is reportedly edible, it appears capable of hybridization with poisonous varieties of *A. pantherina*, and should be avoided. It is moderately common in mixed conifer forests of the Southwest.

Amanita muscaria (Fr.) S. F. Gray

Caps 5–25 cm broad, red to orange-red fading to light reddish orange at the margin, bleaching whitish overall if flushed with rain and sun-dried; gills white and free from the stalk; annulus white and flaring with ragged margins; stalk white, tapering toward the apex; volva white with the margin closely apressed to the stalk with several cottony patches or ringlets extending up the lower part of the stalk; patches of veil tissue randomly distributed or appearing in rings, white and often wartlike in appearance; spore print white. (AMD, LAS, MNA, MSM, SWM)
COMMENTS This is one of the most abundant of all Amanitas in the Southwest. It is common in mixed conifer forests, appearing after summer rains. Those found in spruce-fir forests are often more robust with a darker,

Amanita muscaria

Amanita pantherina

bloodred cap than those in the pine forests. An occasional variety in the Southwest is *A. muscaria* var. *formosa*. It has a yellow to orange buff cap with pale yellow to yellow-tan pigment in the veil remnants and the stalk. (LAS)

Amanita pantherina (DC ex Fr.) Secr.

Caps 2–15 cm broad but usually remaining small, honey yellow to brown at the center with distinct white patches of veil changing in density from the center of the cap to the margin, thin radial lines at the margin; in some caps the pigment fails to develop presenting a nearly white appearance overall; gills white and crowded, slightly attached to the stalk in youth; stalk with a pendant annulus and bandlike residues above the volva; volva separate from the stalk base with an abrupt or rolled margin; spore print white. (LAS, MSM)

COMMENTS   This Amanita is a common associate of conifers, particularly Douglas fir. It is poisonous and because of the variability in its general characteristics and its potential to hybridize with forms of *A. gemmata*, all Amanitas of the group should be avoided.

Amanita pantherina-gemmata hybrid

Fruiting bodies with a combination of characteristics including intermediate coloration of the cap, more or less persistent veil tissue on the cap and stalk, and multiple bands of tissue at the margin of the volva.

COMMENTS   This hybrid is a common associate of ponderosa pine and Douglas fir of the Canadian zone. The reportedly edible *A. rubescens* resembles this hybrid when young. It occurs in the same habitat where oaks and aspen are also present. However, the tissues of *A. rubescens* bruise reddish and the cap turns light reddish brown at maturity. Other distinguishing characteristics include pinkish gray veil patches and a large, white annulus. (LAS, MNA)

Amanita vaginata (Fr.) Vitt.

Caps 4–9 cm broad, conic at first then expanding, variable in color from white, gray, grayish brown to yellow brown, viscid when wet, margin conspicuously *striate*, veil remnants (warts) sometimes present but easily removed; gills free to slightly adnate, thin, white; stalk long and slender tapering from base to apex, base oval or club shaped enclosed in a saclike membranous volva; volva attached only at the base and tearing easily when the fruiting body is removed. (BSM, LAS, MSM)

COMMENTS   Also known as *Amanitopsis vaginata*, this mushroom represents a group of Amanitas that have a membranous volva and lack an annulus. They are common in the Upper Sonoran and Transition zones under pinyon and ponderosa pine. Although others consider them edible, extreme caution is advised because of their variability in this region.

Other Related Species

Amanita inaurata

Caps dark brown with mealy, grayish veil remnants, margin strongly lined; no annulus but with patches of veil tissue on the stalk; volva free from the stalk, saclike. (LAS, MNA)

Limacella glishra

Caps small in relation to stalk length, convex and knobby at the center; annulus as a hairy slimy ring; volva absent; fruiting body covered with copious brown slime. Uncommon and scattered in the spruce-fir forest of Canadian and Hudsonian zones in late summer and early fall. (MNA)

Family Lepiotaceae

Some members of the Lepiotaceae superficially resemble *Amanita* species but they are easily distinguished by the absence of a volva at the base of the stalk and a cap with scales rather than with fragments of veil tissue. Most of the species found in the Southwest are small and resemble miniature parasols. Large Lepiotas are edible with a few notable exceptions. But these are not common in this region, perhaps because they are favored by moist environments. They are typically found in the tropics and wetter areas of the temperate zone. Two of medium size that occur in the Southwest are *Lepiota lutea*, common in greenhouses and gardens (AMD, LAS), and the closely related *Chlorophyllum molybdites*, a green-spored species widely distributed in low-elevation meadows and coniferous forests (described below). Because some of the smaller Lepiotas are considered deadly poisonous, none should ever be eaten.

Amanita pantherina-gemmata

Amanita vaginata

Chlorophyllum molybdites

Chlorophyllum molybdites Mass.

Caps usually large, 8–30 cm broad, strongly convex to cone-shaped, often knobbed at the center, white with numerous buff to cinnamon-colored scales; gills free from the stalk, white becoming grayish to greenish as spores mature; stalk up to 25 cm long and 2.5 cm thick, white staining reddish brown; veil as a persistent membranous ring that is movable on the stalk, fringed at the margin, and discoloring brownish beneath; spore print greenish. (BSM, LAS, MNA, SWM)

COMMENTS   In its early button stage, the poisonous *C. molybdites* is indistinguishable from other species of *Lepiota*. Its green spore print is a distinguishing character and separates it at maturity from its edible look-alike, *Lepiota* (Macrolepiota) *racodes*, which is yet to be reported from this region. (AMD, BSM, LAS, MNA, MSM)

Lepiota clypeolaria (Fr.) Kummer

Caps 2–7 cm broad, ochraceous brown to brown and breaking into scales or patches as the cap expands to expose the lighter creamy-white tissue below, the center raised as a mound and the margin lined with ragged

Lepiota clypeolaria

fragments of veil tissue; gills free from the stalk, white to cream-colored; stalk 6–15 cm long and 1–2.5 cm thick, white at the apex and reddish brown at the base, covered with a woolly pubescence that binds litter fragments to it; spore print white. (LAS, MNA, MSM)

COMMENTS   This is a small, highly variable mushroom that probably represents a complex of related species and varieties. The fruiting bodies appear abundantly in late summer following monsoon rains under pine and Douglas fir of the Transition and Canadian zones. It is suspected to be poisonous.

Family Hygrophoraceae

A single genus, *Hygrophorus*, is traditionally represented in this family of bright-colored, widely distributed mushrooms. However, a number of mycologists recognize *Camarophyllus* and *Hygrocybe* as separate genera on the basis of microscopic differences. The fruiting bodies are mostly small with widely spaced, waxy gills that descend fleshy stalks. A waxy layer will adhere to the fingers if the gills are partially crushed between them. Color is of major importance in the identification of species as are the discoloration and bruising reactions. None are known to be dangerously poisonous but few are eaten because of their slimy caps and small size.

Hygrophorus chrysodon (Fr.) Fries

Caps white, convex to upturned, the center becoming yellow from the accumulation of fine pigment granules, margin thin and wavy; gills white and decurrent on the stalk; stalk slightly viscid, white, with yellow pigment granules near the apex, the tissue turning lemon yellow in a 5 percent solution of potassium hydroxide; spore print white. (AMD, LAS, MNA)

COMMENTS   This species is widely distributed under conifers and is one of the most abundant mushrooms following monsoon rains in the ponderosa pine forest. A look-alike is the slimy capped *H. eburneus*, which lacks yellow pigments and is found in mixed conifer forests and oak woodlands. (LAS, MNA)

Hygrophorus erubescens (Fr.) Fries

Caps broadly convex becoming somewhat raised at the center, whitish to flesh pink and streaked with wine-colored fibrils, the cap tissue bruising

Hygrophorus chrysodon

Hygrophorus erubescens

Hygrophorus pudorinus

yellowish; gills decurrent, widely spaced and thick; stalk whitish pink, narrowing toward the base, length variable according to the variety; spore print white. (SGM)

COMMENTS   This species is quite similar to *H. russula* which has crowded gills and dense reddish purple hairs. (MNA) It is found in groups under conifers, particularly pine, whereas *H. russula* is common under oaks.

Hygrophorus pudorinus Fries

Caps 5–10 cm broad, convex with a wide knob at the center and a wavy margin, slimy with litter debris adhering to the slime, white to pinkish buff or pale flesh color; gills white to pale pink, narrow and descending the stalk at maturity, the tissues staining ochraceous in age; spore print white; odor resinous and taste disagreeable. (AMD, LAS, MSM, SWM)

COMMENTS   Despite its disagreeable flavor, this mushroom is edible when cooked. It grows singly or in groups under spruce and fir and is one of the most abundant fungi in the Canadian and Hudsonian zones in summer and fall. Several varieties exist.

Hygrophorus speciosus Peck

Fruiting bodies single to clustered; cap strongly convex when young becoming broadly convex with a central knob, very slimy when fresh, bright red fading to orange or yellow; gills white or pale yellow, decurrent, edges thick and often yellowed; stalk white, viscid when moist, yellow to orange near the base; veil thin and cobweblike, soon disappearing or leaving a slight ring on the stalk near the apex; spore print white. (AMD, LAS, MNA, MSM, SWM)

COMMENTS   Considerable confusion has arisen regarding the identity of this brightly colored *Hygrophorus*. Formerly it was regarded strictly as a larch associate, but its presence with spruce and pine has been verified. It is particularly common in wet years under ponderosa pine in the Southwest. A look-alike found in association with 2-needled pines and fir is *H. hypothejus*. (LAS) The cap of this species turns olive yellow to dark brown in the center at maturity.

Hygrophorus speciosus

Other Related Species

H. conicus

A delicate reddish to orange species with a conical cap perched atop a thin, fragile stalk. It has a tendency to blacken with age or bruising. It is widely distributed and common. (LAS, MSM)

H. eburneus

A Hygrophorus with a white to ivory cap, usually covered with copious slime and white gills decurrent on a white stalk. Found in the Transition zone in mixed pine and oak.

H. subalpinus

A white, robust species found at the edge of melting snowbanks in the Canadian zone and at the margins of the Alpine tundra. (MSM)

Family Russulaceae

The collective characteristics that set this family apart from all other gilled mushrooms include: caps with uplifted margins and an easily removable cuticle; brittle flesh which is easily crushed; absence of veils; a black to bluish-black color reaction (*amyloid*) of the hymenial tissue upon the application of an iodine solution; and an *acrid* or bitter taste in many of the species. There are only two genera in the family, *Russula* and *Lactarius*. The caps of many *Russula* species are brightly and variously colored but unfortunately they are difficult to identify without the use of microscopic features. This is particularly true of the red-capped russulas. Southwestern members of the Russulaceae have received little attention by mycologists in the past, and it is quite likely that new species will be discovered and described in the future.

The principal character of *Lactarius* is the presence of clear or colored fluid (latex), which is exuded from the cut or broken tissues of the fruiting body. This latex, which characteristically separates it from *Russula* sp., is best observed in the gill tissue of young specimens growing under moist conditions. Latex may not be exhibited under dry conditions. Some members of both genera have a peppery to acrid taste. Placing the tissues in contact with the tongue can produce a burning sensation. Taste is an important character for the identification of species, as is the color of the

Lactarius alnicola

cap and stalk and whether or not these are viscid. Species known to be poisonous are often those with a disagreeable taste. Because of the difficulty in identification, these species should be regarded with caution on the first try at eating them. They must not be eaten unless well cooked, and probably should not be eaten at all.

Both *Russula* and *Lactarius* are parasitized by the Ascomycete fungus, *Hypomyces*. They retain their general shape upon parasitism but the entire fruiting body is often covered with an orange-red to green hyphal mat. The parasitic relationship of *Hypomyces* with *R. brevipes* is illustrated below.

Lactarius alnicola group

Caps 8–15 cm broad, widely funnel-shaped at maturity, yellow-ocher overall, paler at the margin and somewhat zoned, finely hairy with litter debris often adhering to the surface; latex scant, clear, and staining tissues yellow or not at all; gills decurrent, ochraceous-buff and staining darker yellow-brown where bruised; stalk dry, white above ochraceous at the base, hollow with surrounding tissues firm, conspicuous small cavities or depressions on the surface (*scrobiculate*); spore print white to pale buff;

taste slowly but distinctly acrid. (AMD, LAS)

COMMENTS   Although the name of this group of related species indicates an association with alder, their distribution seems to indicate a strong affinity for conifers, and particularly pines. Our southwestern variety has only scant latex. The related *L. scrobiculatus* has a light yellow to orange-yellow cap with a zoned, woolly surface, a stalk that is distinctly pitted with honey-colored spots, and the latex from the cut gills is white at first quickly changing to sulfur yellow. *L. scrobiculatus* also occurs with pine in southern Colorado. (LAS, MNA, MSM) *Lactarius* species, which have latex that turn yellow, should be considered poisonous and should not be eaten.

Lactarius barrowsii Smith

Caps 2–10 cm broad, whitish to light pinkish cinnamon when young, moist with an inrolled margin that expands in age; the center depressed and colored ochraceous orange with occasional flushes of greenish gray; gills narrow and crowded, ochraceous to pinkish orange with a greenish cast, exuding a limited red latex where cut; flesh quickly changing to green on exposure; stalk concolorous with cap and both covered with a whitish or velvety bloom when young; spore deposit yellowish; taste mild and slightly fruity.

COMMENTS   This species has been reported only from the Southwest. It is found in pinyon-juniper woodlands and under ponderosa pine, appearing after late summer and fall monsoon rains. I have found it to be edible and good.

Lactarius sp. (near *chelidonium*)

Caps 4–12 cm broad, broadly convex with center depressed at maturity, the margin inrolled when young, off-white becoming rosy buff, orange buff, or flesh-colored; margin uneven and wavy at maturity, zoned or uniformly colored, pale green or blue-green showing from below; latex scant, dull orange to light ochraceous, brown later changing to green or blue-green; gills cream-colored to pale ochraceous buff, decurrent on the stalk; stalk short with a narrow base, colored as the gills; odor pleasantly aromatic; taste slightly bitter.

COMMENTS   As a member of the subgenus *deliciosus* this undescribed species resembles *L. chelidonium* primarily in the color of its latex and cap

Lactarius barrowsii

Lactarius sp.

Lactarius deliciosus

Lactarius indigo

tissues. In some specimens the entire fruiting body turns blue-green to blue reminiscent of the color of *L. indigo.* Its edibility is unknown and because of the slightly bitter flavor, it is not recommended. It is a very common mushroom under pines in the Transition zone and is found in combination with *Russula brevipes* and *L. alnicola.*

Lactarius deliciosus (Fr.) S. F. Gray

Caps 5–14 cm broad, convex to depressed at the center, margin inrolled, viscid to sticky at first, soon dry, colored carrot orange mixed with tones of vinaceous red, salmon, and green; sometimes colored in faint zones, usually becoming more green with age especially at the margin; surface occasionally breaking up to form a network of patches when dry; flesh thick, pale orange-buff, slowly staining vinaceous; latex scant and carrot-colored leaving green stains; gills attached to decurrent on stalk, orange but quickly stained vinaceous red, finally entirely green in age; stalk 2.5 cm long, 1.5–3 cm thick, light orange turning green in age. (AMD, BSM, LAS, MSM, MNA)
COMMENTS   Found scattered or clustered under mixed conifers in the wetter sites of the Transition, Canadian, and Hudsonian zones, this species is similar to *L. rubrilacteus* but its latex is orange. The most frequently encountered variety in the Southwest is that described by A. H. Smith as *L. deliciosus* var. *areolatus.*

Lactarius indigo (Schw.) Fr.

Caps 5–15 cm broad, margin inrolled in youth, indigo blue when fresh and fading silvery blue-green; flesh pallid to bluish; gills descending the stalk, close, indigo blue but fading in age; stalk colored as the cap and gills; spore print yellow. (AMD, LAS, MNA)
COMMENTS   Found under pine and mixed pine-oak forests following monsoon rain, this brilliantly colored Lactarius is edible and very good.

Lactarius representaneus Britz.

Caps 3–15 cm broad, convex with inrolled margin becoming vase-shaped, the margin densely hairy or bearded, unzoned, yellow to orange yellow including hairs; flesh white staining dull lilac or purplish where cut or bruised; latex abundant, white to cream turning lilac to violet; gills at-

Lactarius representaneus

tached and decurrent on stipe, cream to orange buff; stalk even to some-what club-shaped, surface sticky, pitted with orange spots; taste acrid. (LAS, MNA)

COMMENTS   Easily recognized by its bearded cap and orange-yellow cap this Lactarius occurs under spruce and fir in the Hudsonian zone. It is reportedly poisonous.

Lactarius rubrilacteus A. H. Smith

Caps 6–12 cm broad, funnel-shaped at maturity, viscid when wet, develop-ing a rich carrot color with distinct zones of lighter orange and greenish flushes in age; latex orange-red to bloodred; gills thin and crowded, not strongly decurrent, light pinkish cinnamon becoming dull pinkish red with green stains; spore print cream-colored. (AMD, SGM, MSM)

COMMENTS   This species fruits in summer and early fall under Douglas fir and mixed conifer forests in the Canadian zone. It is closely related to, and may actually be the European species, *L. sanguifluus*. Fruiting abundantly in moist years, it is edible and good.

Lactarius rubrilacteus

Lactarius rufus group

Lactarius rufus group

Caps 1.5–5 cm broad, the margin inrolled, expanding to flat or shallowly depressed, smooth or inconspicuously hairy, rufous-orange to orange cinnamon on drying; flesh white to pinkish cinnamon, fragile; gills slightly decurrent, pale pinkish cinnamon, moderately broad in long and short tiers; latex milk white, unchanging; stalk colored as the gills but becoming concolorous with the cap, lighter in color at the base; taste slowly and strongly acrid. (MSM)

COMMENTS   This species is likely a variant of *Lactarius rufus* (LAS, MNA) which is poisonous. A number of similarly colored, small Lactarii in the section Russularia resemble this species including *R. luculentus*. (MSM) It is found at high elevations associated with spruce and bristlecone pine in the Hudsonian zone.

Lactarius uvidus (Fr.) Fries

Caps 3–10 cm broad with the naked margin inrolled at first becoming flat or uplifted in age, a slight knob in the center; faint color zones or uniformly pale brownish-lilac to wine-colored brown; gills partly descending the stalk, white, bruising lilac or purple; latex white staining tissues purple; stalk of equal thickness, white with pale lilac stains; taste bitter. (BSM, LAS, MNA)

COMMENTS   The southwestern *L. uvidus* is probably variety *montanus* as described by Smith. It is common in gregarious clusters under conifers of the Canadian and Hudsonian zones. Like all purple-staining Lactarii, it should not be eaten.

Russula alutacea group

Caps 6–12 cm broad, convex and becoming depressed at the center with a wavy, slightly striate margin, colored orange-red, rose-red, to dark-red overall but fading to straw-yellow or off-white at the center; gills attached, white becoming straw-colored; stalk white, rarely developing pink or reddish color; spore print light yellow to ocher-yellow; tastes weakly to strongly acrid. (AMD)

COMMENTS   This species is a member of one of the most abundant Russula species complexes found in the southwestern ponderosa pine forest.

Lactarius uvidus

Russula alutacea

Because of its peppery or acrid taste, it is not considered edible. Fruiting bodies are found individually or growing in arcs beneath or emerging from the needle layer following monsoon rains. The *Russula maculata* group is similar in appearance but is primarily associated with hardwoods.

Russula brevipes Pk.

Caps 5–15 cm broad, broadly convex to markedly depressed at the center, dry and minutely woolly, white and tinged with yellow-brown in age, margin inrolled at first becoming expanded; gills white usually alternating long with short, attached and descending the stalk, stained cinnamon brown in age; stalk white becoming stained like the gills, thick at the apex and tapering toward the base, apex occasionally tinged blue-green; odor of formic acid and slightly disagreeable; taste slightly acrid or peppery. (BSM, LAS, MNA, MSM)

COMMENTS   *R. brevipes* is similar and perhaps identical to the European species, *R. delica*. It is the most common white-colored *Russula* in the southwestern pine forests. In mid-summer and throughout the fall it emerges from below the needle litter raising it up in conspicuous mounds. In dry periods it develops and fruits below the litter. Because of this fruiting habit, the cap tissue is often covered with soil and litter fragments that are difficult to remove. Although edible, it has a slightly peppery taste with little mushroom flavor and a coarse texture. White-colored look-alikes are *R. nigricans* and *R. albonigra*, but the tissue of these species turns black on bruising and on aging. (LAS, MNA, MSM)

Russula emetica (Fr.) Pers.

Caps 5–15 cm broad, bright red above a chalk-white flesh, slightly viscid or tacky, margin even and striate when fully expanded; gills attached, pure white or slightly cream-colored in age, closely spaced; stalk white without pinkish or reddish stains; taste strongly and quickly acrid. (BSM, LAS, MNA, MSM)

COMMENTS   Red-colored russulas are difficult to distinguish microscopically and they are often mistakenly considered to be this species. The acrid taste, chalk-white gills, and white spore print are distinctive characters. *R. emetica* contains gastrointestinal irritants and eating it would be a painful

Russula brevipes and orange parasite

Russula emetica

mistake. It is found scattered about in shady, moist sites beneath high-elevation conifers of the Hudsonian zone, often emerging from a moss-covered humus layer.

Russula rosacea (Pers. ex Secr.) Fries

Caps 5–9 cm broad, convex to broadly convex and occasionally depressed at the center; margin smooth and wavy, bright shiny red that fades rose-red; gills white to light cream or yellow, attached and slightly descending on the stalk; stalk smooth white becoming flushed rosy-red to reddish, the color sometimes covering the entire surface; spore print white to cream; taste moderately to strongly acrid. (AMD, LAS, MSM)

COMMENTS   Also known as *R. sanguineus*, this species is associated with pine in the Transition and Upper Sonoran zones and occasionally with other conifers. Its flesh is extremely brittle and crushes easily when transported. It is reportedly poisonous and has an unpleasant acrid taste. A look-alike is the scarlet variety of *R. xerampelina* that has a shellfishlike odor and a mild taste. (AMD, MSM)

Other common russulas

R. aeruginea

Cap greenish with yellowish gills and spore print. Associated with aspen and pines. (LAS)

R. claroflava

Cap yellow with ocher gills, and white flesh that grays on bruising. Found in aspen and mixed conifer forests. Also known as *R. flava*. (LAS, MNA)

Family Tricholomataceae

By the process of elimination, mushrooms with white spore prints that do not meet the criteria for the previously discussed white-spored families (Amanitaceae, Lepiotaceae, Hygrophoraceae, Russulaceae), are classified here in the Tricholomataceae. The family is the largest of the gilled mushrooms and is frustratingly diverse. It has been referred to by other authors as a "dumping ground" for the nondescript mushrooms. Only those genera containing species which are frequently and consistently represented in the

Russula rosacea

southwestern mycoflora are included here. You are referred to other guides for a broader treatment. Some genera not treated here but included elsewhere are *Asterophora, Cystoderma, Lentinellus, Leptoglossum, Lyophyllum, Melanoleuca, Omphalina, Omphalotus, Panellus, Panus,* and *Trogia.* Features which generally characterize the whole family include: attached, often crowded gills; tissue in the stalk that is continuous with the cap so that the stalk and cap are not easily separated; and lack of a volva.

Genera of the Tricholomataceae may be grouped according to common features of the fruiting body. Veil remnants on the stalk occur in all or some members of the genera *Armillaria, Armillariella, Cystoderma, Lentinus, Pleurotus,* and *Tricholoma.* Wood inhabiting species with reduced stalks or stalks absent are found in the genera *Lentinus, Pleurotus,* and *Phyllotopsis.* These three genera resemble the Polypores and allied wood decay fungi but they have fleshy fruiting bodies as opposed to fruiting bodies which are tough, leathery or woody. Fleshy, stalked genera which arise from the ground (rarely from wood) include *Tricholoma, Clitocybe,* and *Leucopaxillus.* Genera with members that typically possess very thin cartilaginous stalks that arise from either wood or the ground include *Cystoderma,*

Armillaria albolanaripes

Armillaria straminea var. americana

Collybia, *Marasmius*, and *Mycena*. A positive amyloid reaction (a bluish-black color) of the spore mass to a solution of iodine is helpful in the identification of some species in the genera *Armillaria*, *Clitocybe*, *Hygrophoropsis*, *Leucopaxillus*, *Phyllotopsis*, *Pleurotus*, and *Mycena*.

The genera and species of the Tricholomataceae are presented in alphabetical order in the descriptions which follow.

Armillaria albolanaripes Atkinson

Cap lemon-yellow to orange-yellow becoming dingy yellow-brown, with conspicuous flattened brown scales, 8–15 cm broad, convex with a whitish inrolled margin; gills separate, torn at the margin, adnexed (notched), white becoming cream-colored in age; stalk even, shiny, white to light yellow-brown, with one to several cottony zones of veil remnants. (AMD, LAS, MNA, MSM, SWM)
COMMENTS   As a species of common occurrence in the Canadian zone in late summer and fall, *A. albolanaripes* (classified by some as *Floccularia albolinaripes*) resembles a *Pholiota*, but it has light colored gills and a white spore print which is weakly amyloid. It is edible but lacks the quality of its relative *A. straminea*.

Armillaria straminea var. *americana* Mit. & A. H. Smith

Caps 4–15 cm broad, conical when young becoming flat; margins uplifted in age with remnants of yellow veil; surface white becoming straw yellow, covered with dark yellow fibrous scales arranged in concentric circles, color fading with age; gills broad, close, pale yellow becoming lemon yellow, attached to the stalk; stalk 1.5–2 cm thick, smooth and white above a yellowish cottony ring, scaly like the pileus below. (LAS)
COMMENTS   This robust Armillaria is abundant at times in southern Colorado and northern New Mexico, growing in association with aspen-mixed conifer forests of the Canadian zone.

Armillaria zelleri Stuntz & Smith

Caps 5–15 cm broad, convex with inrolled margin, viscid to tacky, orange brown fibrils overlying whitish yellow, olive yellow flesh; gills attached, whitish, staining rusty brown; stalk firm, 1.0–2.5 cm thick tapering to a pointed base, sheathed with fibrils from the base up to the ragged ring; ring orange below and white above; odor and taste mealy. (LAS, MNA, MSM)

COMMENTS   This is a widely distributed species associated with pine and aspen. It is classified by some as *Tricholoma zelleri*. The similar appearing *A. ponderosa* (*T. magnivelare*), is the choice edible white matsutake. Unlike *A. zelleri*, the matsutake has a distinctive spicy odor and a much more agreeable flavor. It has been collected in southern Colorado and can be expected to occur in Arizona, New Mexico, and Mexico. (AMD, LAS, MNA, MSM)

Armillariella mellea (Fr.) Karsten

Caps 3–15 cm broad, convex becoming plane, often knobbed in the center, with the margin uplifted in age; surface viscid to tacky when wet, usually with scattered erect dark brown hairs or scales over the center; color extremely variable but generally yellow, honey yellow or pinkish brown in age; gills attached or slightly decurrent on the stalk, whitish when young then yellowish to pinkish, flesh color or brown in age; stalk 5–20 cm long, 0.5–2.0 cm thick, fibrous, whitish, discoloring yellowish to grayish tan or rust brown especially below the ring; ring cottony, membranous, white to yellowish, persistent on upper stalk. (AMD, BSM, LAS, MNA, MSM, SWM)

COMMENTS   The "Honey Mushroom" as this species is known, is widely distributed and found growing on decaying wood or on the ground arising from buried wood debris of both hardwood and conifers. In the Southwest it is particularly abundant in the wetter sites of the Canadian and Hudsonian zones which have been opened by timber harvest. Also classified as *Armillaria mellea* it often grows in massive clusters with the stalks fused at the base. The caps are edible and good.

Clitocybe gibba (Fr.) Kummer

Caps 3–8 cm broad, pinkish tan fading to brownish tan, with sunken center becoming funnel-shaped, smooth, with an even to wavy margin; gills crowded, forked, chalky white to gray buff, descending the stalk; stalk thin, 4–12 mm thick, equal, smooth, occasionally with a dense woolly base; spore print white; spores nonamyloid. (LAS, MNA)

COMMENTS   Another name for this species is *C. infundibuliformis*. It is a very common mushroom of mixed oak and pine stands in the Transition

Armillaria zelleri

Armillariella mellea

Clitocybe gibba

zone, fruiting abundantly in late summer and fall. It has a coarse texture but is reported to be edible.

Clitocybe gibba var. *maxima* (Fr.) Bigelow

Cap 4–10 cm broad, flat becoming broadly funnel-shaped, smooth, somewhat scaly at the center, flesh color to pinkish tan; gills cream to pinkish tan, narrow, crowded, long-decurrent on the stalk; stalk 1–1.15 cm thick, whitish to pale flesh color; spore print white; spores nonamyloid; odor pronounced. (SGM)

COMMENTS   This is a more robust variety of *C. gibba*, and it appears to be associated more closely with oak in the Transition zone. It is common following monsoon rains in late summer and early fall in mixed pine and oak stands.

Clitocybe gibba var. maxima

Other Common Clitocybes

C. dilatata

As a conspicuous whitish species with a wavy cap margin and growing in dense clusters along roadways in conifer forests, *C. dilatata* is considered to be poisonous. (LAS, MNA, MSM)

C. odora

This Clitocybe is distinctive because of its blue-green color and aniselike odor. It is found widely scattered in mixed conifer and aspen hardwood stands of the Canadian and Hudsonian zones. It is a poor quality edible. (LAS, MNA, MSM, SWM)

Flammulina velutipes (Curt. ex Fr.) Singer

Caps 2–6 cm broad, convex with margin inrolled, pale orange yellow at the margin and orange red to pinkish cinnamon at the center; gills adnexed (notched), widely spaced, broad, cream to yellow; stalk 1–10 cm long ×

Flammulina velutipes

3–7 mm thick, yellowish at the apex, covered with dense velvety brown to blackish brown hairs at the base, hollow at maturity, flesh tough; spore print white; spores nonamyloid. (AMD, LAS, MNA, MSM)

COMMENTS   This species is very common on decayed aspen wood fruiting in clusters in late fall and winter. The caps are edible if well cooked but the stems should be discarded.

Hygrophoropsis aurantiaca (Fr.) Maire

Fruiting body uniformly orange to brownish orange; cap darkens with age, 2–8 cm broad, velvety on the surface, flesh thin, margin inrolled and wavy; gills crowded, blunt-edged, and prominently forked near the cap margin, decurrent on the stalk; stalk 3–7 cm long, thickened toward the base, distinct from the cap, attachment central to slightly lateral; spore print white to cream colored. (AMD, LAS, MNA, MSM)

COMMENTS   This attractive brightly colored mushroom (classified by some authors in the Paxillaceae) was formerly known as *Clitocybe aurantiaca*. It is considered by some to be poisonous although there are many

Hygrophoropsis aurantiaca

records of its edibility. Because it resembles the small edible fruiting bodies of the chanterelle, *Cantharellus cibarius*, collections should be carefully examined when taken from pine and Douglas fir stands where both species occur. The most definitive characteristics of the false chanterelle are the thin forked gills and whitish spore print.

Laccaria laccata (Fr.) Berk. & Br.

Cap 1–4 cm broad, convex to flat, margin uplifted and wavy at maturity, color variable, flesh-colored, reddish tan or pinkish ocher; gills broad, thick, widely separated, flesh color to pink, attached, and slightly decurrent on the stalk, somewhat waxy; stalk slender, nearly equal, tissues often twisted, colored like the cap; spore print white. (AMD, LAS, MNA, MSM, SWM)

COMMENTS   The overall appearance of this mushroom is highly variable and in some forms, it is similar to small species of *Hygrophorus*. There are several similarly colored species that are widespread throughout the forests

Laccaria laccata

Lentinus ponderosus

of the Southwest particularly under conifers. *L. amethystina* is a brilliantly violet colored species. (AMD, LAS) Laccarias are not known to be poisonous but they seem to be rather tasteless.

Lentinus ponderosus O.K. Miller

Caps 10–50 cm broad, depressed centrally, white to yellowish cream colored, surface dry covered with conspicuous, broad wood brown scales that are curled at maturity; gills white to cream colored, characteristically torn or split (serrated) at the edges, firm like the flesh of the cap and drying hard, decurrent; stalk central to slightly lateral, widest at the apex, narrowed to a tough woody rootlike base, lacking veil tissue; spore print white; odor sweet. (LAS)

COMMENTS   Very few gilled mushrooms in our region reach the size of this species. It is moderately abundant following monsoon rains in the summer and fall in mixed stands of ponderosa pine and Douglas fir. Some specimens have a fragrant, spicy odor. Its flesh is tough and Miller recommends considerable cooking to render it edible. (MNA) It is definitely chewy under any circumstances. A similar species, *L. lepideus*, is common on logs and stumps of aspen and various conifers. It is much smaller with dark reddish brown scales and a prominent apical ring on the stalk. (LAS, MNA) A related conifer wood inhabiting mushroom, *Lentinellus ursinus*, lacks a stalk, has a lobed fan-shaped cap with thick brown hairs and serrated gills. (BSM, LAS, MNA)

Leucopaxillus albissimus (A. & S.) Kuhner

Caps 3–20 cm broad, convex to nearly flat with inrolled margin when young; chalk white discoloring to pale yellowish to yellowish tan toward the center, splitting and cracking in age; gills attached and often partly descending the stalk, white; stalk 5–10 cm long and 1–3 cm thick, swollen at the base, smooth, white, a dense mat of white mycelium at the base. (BSM, LAS, MNA, MSM)

COMMENTS   This robust, attractive, white species is too bitter to eat and some have reported it to be indigestible. It is illustrated here with the brown-capped *L. amarus* for comparison. *L. albissimus* fruits under conifers, particularly Douglas fir in the Canadian zone.

*Leucopaxillus **albissimus*** and *Leucopaxillus amarus*

Leucopaxillus amarus

Leucopaxillus amarus (A. & S.) Kuhner

Cap 5–12 cm broad, brown to reddish brown, lighter at the inrolled margin, convex to flat, center sometimes raised, surface smooth, dry; gills adnate, closely spaced, white; stalk equal to swollen at the base, white with brown tints at the base where bruised, arising singly or in clusters from a dense, white basal mycelium; spore print white. (AMD, LAS, MNA, MSM, SWM)

COMMENTS   Also known as *L. gentianeus* this robust mushroom fruits in the needle and leaf litter beneath pines and oak. The copious white mycelial mat below the fruiting bodies and the strongly bitter taste are characteristics also shared by the pure white species, *L. albissimus.*

Mycena alcalina (Fr.) Kummer

Caps 1–4 cm broad, broadly conic to bell shaped, margin lightly striate, color grayish brown with a whitish surface bloom becoming brown at the center; gills attached and ascending, whitish to pinkish gray staining red-brown in age; stalk 1–3 mm thick, brown to gray brown, shiny, with a basal swelling; odor alkaline; taste acrid. (MNA)

COMMENTS   One of the distinguishing characters of this common Mycena is its bleachlike (alkaline) odor when crushed. It grows on conifer wood and needles. Its edibility is unknown.

Mycena alcalina

Mycena pura

Mycena pura (Fr.) Quellet

Cap 1–4 cm broad, conic to broadly convex, color variable and mixed, generally lilac or purplish but also tinged with white, pink, rosy red or blue; cap margin striate when young; gills broad, attached, equally spaced, colored as the cap with unpigmented edges; stalk 2–6 mm thick, equal to enlarged at the base, tissues often twisted; spore print white. (LAS, MNA, MSM)

COMMENTS   *Mycena pura* is one of the more distinctly colored Mycenas and has a definite radishlike flavor. It is also suspected to be poisonous. There are over 300 species of *Mycena*, and many occur in the Southwest. They are very difficult to identify. Collectively they are small, fragile, fleshy mushrooms found as saprophytes on plant litter. They often occur in troops but their small size makes them uninteresting as potential edibles.

Phyllotopsis nidulans

Phyllotopsis nidulans (Pers. ex Fr.) Singer

Fruiting body stalkless and attached to wood; caps 2–5 cm broad, orange but bleaching whitish, surface covered with a cottony pubescence, margin inrolled and often split; gills orange to orange yellow, radiating outward from the margin to a narrow point of attachment on wood; spore print pinkish; odor strong and disagreeable. (BSM, LAS, MNA, SWM)

COMMENTS   Previously classified with *Pleurotus* and *Panellus*, *P. nidulans* is widespread on both aspen and conifers. It is not known to be poisonous but its odor is strong and disagreeable.

Pleurotus ostreatus Fr.

Cap 2–25 cm broad, fan-shaped, semicircular to elongate, white to pale brown, surface smooth, margin lobed and wavy in some specimens; gills white to yellowish, not crowded, decurrent on the stalk if present; stalk short, lateral, off center or absent, white to yellowish in age; spore print white. (AMD, LAS, MNA, MSM, SWM)

Pleurotus ostreatus

COMMENTS   Known as the "Oyster" mushroom because of its shelllike appearance, *P. ostreatus* is edible and choice. I have successfully introduced my students to mycophagy with young specimens of this mushroom. Its popularity has promoted its appearance in the supermarkets. The clustered caps can be found on deciduous trees of the Riparian zone, on aspen and occasionally pine in the Canadian and Hudsonian zones. A number of white to brown relatives of this species have been collected including *P. sapidus* (with a violet spore print) and *P. elongatipes* (with an elongated stalk). (MNA) The bitter *Lentinellus ursinus* may be mistaken for an over-mature *Pleurotus* but it has a densely hairy, soft, fan-shaped cap bearing pinkish brown gills with serrated margins. (BSM, LAS)

Tricholoma pardinum Quellet

Caps 5–10 cm broad, convex to plane, often with a central knob, dry, white, covered with many small patches of gray brown to gray hairy scales or fibrils, scales most dense at the center, margin uneven; gills white, creamy white, sometimes flushed with pink, wavy; stalk chalky white,

Tricholoma pardinum

smooth, equal or enlarged near the base, sometimes with rusty stains at the base; spore print white; odor of fresh meat or mealy. (LAS, MNA, MSM, SWM)

COMMENTS   This very poisonous *Tricholoma* is abundant in mixed conifer-hardwood forests but with sporadic fruiting from year to year. As a rule of thumb, all white to gray brown species should be avoided because of their potential toxicity. *T. terreum* is a similar species with brownish gray scales over a white background. It is found in the fall in this region under pinyon pine and occasionally under other conifers of the Transition zone.

Tricholoma saponaceum (Fr.) Kummer

Caps 3−8 cm broad, convex to plane, the surface cracking to form platelike scales when dry, surface smooth, sticky to viscid, olive to gray or yellowish olive, sometimes with a low, central knob; gills widely spaced, white to cream, sometimes with a pinkish or greenish tint; stalk white or colored as the cap, flesh of the base pinkish, bruising pink or brownish overall; spore print white; odor of soap; taste mildly of soap. (LAS, MNA, MSM)

Tricholoma saponaceum

Tricholomopsis platyphylla

COMMENTS   This species is common in coniferous forests where it is particularly abundant in pine and fir stands. It fruits in the fall and should not be eaten.

Tricholomopsis platyphylla (Fr.) Singer

Caps 5–20 cm broad, convex becoming flat in age, surface smooth, dry, lacking hairs or hairs at the center, blackish brown to gray or whitish gray; margin inrolled at first; gills attached, widely spaced and very broad (deep), white to gray; stalk 6–12 cm long, 1–3 cm thick, equal or swollen at the base, white to grayish white, firm and hollow in age, conspicuous white rhizomorphs at the base; veil absent. (LAS, MNA)

COMMENTS   Recognized by its grayish brown cap, white stalk and broad gills, *T. platyphylla* grows on or near wood of hardwoods in the Riparian zone. Its flavor as an edible is poor, and some people have suffered from digestive upset after eating it.

Tricholomopsis rutilans (Fr.) Singer

Caps 3–10 cm broad, yellow below a dense covering of bright purplish red hairs; gills attached and notched, yellow, broad and crowded; stalk up to 2

Tricholomopsis rutilans

cm thick, yellow with reddish or reddish purple hairs, flesh bruising yellow; veil absent; spore print white. (LAS, MNA, MSM, SWM)

COMMENTS   Often produced singly or sometimes in clusters on conifer wood, this colorful species fruits in summer and fall. It is reportedly edible but of poor quality.

Xeromphalina campanella (Fr.) Kuhner & Maire

Cap 0.3–2.5 cm broad, convex with a sunken center, dull yellowish orange to orange brown, margin lined and inrolled when young; gills thick, widely spaced with lateral connecting veins, yellow to reddish orange becoming orange brown, descending the stalk; stalk 1–4 cm long, very thin, tough and pliant, with dark brown hairs at the base; the stalks often fused together to produce tight clusters; spore print white to cream colored. (AMD, LAS, MNA)

COMMENTS   This beautiful miniature mushroom is widespread, fruiting in large clumps on decayed stumps and logs. It is specifically associated with conifers. Edibility is unknown.

Xeromphalina campanella

Family Coprinaceae

Some authors consider members of this family the "weeds" of the mushroom world. Certainly they are found in the habitats we are likely to frequent, such as parks, lawns, meadows, and cultivated land. In the large genus *Coprinus*, the handsomely proportioned, bell-shaped cap is rapidly transformed into an inky black liquid, thus prompting the common name of "Inky Caps." Of the nearly two hundred species, most are small and found on dung and organic debris. Two related and widely distributed genera, *Psathyrella* and *Panaeolus* do not liquefy, but do have a black to dark brown spore print and bell-shaped cap. Unlike *Coprinus*, their gills are attached to the stalk. The fruiting bodies of the majority of the family are small and fragile and not substantial enough for eating. *Panaeolus foenisecii* (MNA) is a common lawn-inhabiting mushroom and *P. campanulatus* (LAS) is found in cow dung. A number of members contain toxins and trace amounts of hallucinogens, thereby endowing them with an undeserved popularity. A related family, the Bolbitiaceae, contains members intermediate between the Coprinaceae and the Cortinariaceae. None have been included in this guide because of their small stature and nondescript nature.

Coprinus atramentarius (Fr.) Singer

Caps 4–6 cm broad, longer than broad, oval when young becoming conical to bell-shaped, surface glabrous or silky at first developing small brown scales at the center; grayish brown to gray or inky gray in age; margins scalloped, turning black and splitting in age; gills free from stalk, white becoming brownish, then black, stalk 8–15 cm tall, 0.6–1.2 cm thick, white except for grayish to brownish veil fibers at the base; veil tissue as a basal ring or inconspicuous volva. (LAS, MNA, MSM, SWM)
COMMENTS   Like the shaggy mane, this species is edible but when consumed with alcohol can produce illness. It is found clustered on or near stumps, decayed logs, or buried wood. It is extremely common and widespread, fruiting in both spring and fall.

Coprinus atramentarius

Coprinus comatus

Coprinus comatus (Fr.) S. F. Gray

Fruiting body white, robust with a bell-shaped cap 5–12 cm tall and covered with large conspicuous white to light brown scales; gills free, crowded together, white becoming progressively black from the lower margins toward the top of the cap; stalk white with veil tissue as a ring on the lower part; spore print black. (AMD, LAS, MNA, MSM)

COMMENTS   *C. comatus*, because of its prominent scales on the cap, is known commonly as "Shaggy Mane." It grows in clusters, sometimes in great abundance, along margins of roadways, paths, or scattered in open grassy areas. Similar species are *C. micaceus*, with glistening granules on a light brown cap (LAS, MNA, MSM, SWM) and *C. atramentarius* (LAS). The shaggy mane is edible and choice.

Psathyrella circellatipes Benoist

Fruiting bodies clustered, thin, and fragile; caps conic to convex, smooth and moist with inconspicuous vertical lines that fade as the cap matures; gills attached but later free; spore print grayish brown. (SGM)

Psathyrella circellatipes

COMMENTS   Some years, this mushroom grows very abundantly in late summer and fall. It is associated with aspen in the moist sites of the Transition and Canadian zones. Its edibility is not established and because of the close relationship of this genus to poisonous members of the Strophariaceae it is best not to eat it. A related species is *P. hydrophila* with a white stalk and veil remnants on a dark brown cap margin. The gills have beaded droplets when young. It occurs in dense clusters on wood and it is widely distributed. (AMD, SGM)

Family Gomphidiaceae

The dark gray to black spores and widely spaced decurrent gills are diagnostic characteristics for this family. There are two genera found in the Southwest, *Chroogomphus* and *Gomphidius*. Both are common as mycorrhizal associates of conifers, particularly pine species. A partially hypogeous relative of *Chroogomphus*, discussed in the section on Agaricoid Gasteromycetes, is *Brauniellula nancyae*, which is also a mycorrhizal associate of pine.

Chroogomphus vinicolor (Pk.) Miller

Cap 1–6 cm broad, convex to turban-shaped with the margin turned down, ochraceous brown to reddish brown with strong wine-colored hues, sticky to viscid, drying shiny; gills broad, thick, ocher with wine-colored stains, turning blackish in age, decurrent; stalk long and slender, often tapered downward, orange to wine-colored or reddish orange, flesh orange; veil remnant as a wispy hairy ring; spore print smoky gray to black. (LAS)

COMMENTS   This species is common and widely distributed in conifer forests. In the fall during dry periods it can be found beneath the needle layer under ponderosa and lodgepole pine. Rodents eat it, but it is avoided by fungus flies. A closely related look-alike is *C. rutilus*, a larger, brown-colored species. One needs to determine microscopic characters to separate them. (LAS, MSM, SWM)

Gomphidius glutinosus Fries

Cap 2–8 cm broad, convex to flat, margin inrolled at first, then upturned, slimy, brown to purplish brown or reddish brown, staining blackish; gills decurrent, white becoming gray; stalk up to 2 cm thick; tapering toward a

Chroogomphus vinicolor

Gomphidius glutinosus

yellow-colored base; veil as a slimy ring which darkens from the black spores. (LAS, MNA, SWM)

COMMENTS   This Gomphidius resembles a *Hygrophorus* but it is readily recognized by its black spore print. It is typically a high-elevation species and is associated with conifers, especially spruce and subalpine fir in the Hudsonian zone.

Gomphidius subroseus Kauffman

Cap 4–6 cm broad, convex to flat, a copious slime layer on the surface, rosy pink becoming whitish at the margin; gills widely spaced, thick, waxy, white becoming grayish at maturity, decurrent; stalk tapering toward the base, white above and lemon yellow at the base, with a slimy ring that collects the dark spores as they are released; spore print smoky gray to black. (LAS, MNA, MSM)

COMMENTS   *G. subroseus* is one of the colorful mushrooms found in the Transition and Canadian zones where it is associated with ponderosa pine and Douglas fir. If the cap is peeled away before cooking, it is edible and good.

Gomphidius subroseus

Family Agaricaceae

The family is a small one, containing only three genera of which the genus *Agaricus* is best known and most widely represented in the Southwest. The commercially grown *A. brunnescens* and the closely related meadow mushroom *A. campestris* are choice edibles but are not often encountered in this region. Members of Agaricus can be readily recognized by the following features: cap separable from the stalk, gills free from the stalk at maturity, the stalk with a more or less persistent ring but no volva or cup at the base, gills whitish gray to salmon pink when young becoming dark chocolate brown with a similarly colored spore print. Species are grouped on the basis of the staining reaction of tissues when bruised, that is, a yellow or a pink to reddish color change as compared to no change at all. Other diagnostic characteristics include type of ring, general stature of the fruiting body, and odor. Some species are mildly poisonous and since species are difficult to identify on field characters alone, one should exercise caution in eating them. However, *Agaricus* is the most popular group of edible mushroom and because of their general availability in a variety of habitats, it is worthwhile becoming familiar with the edible species. I have found Arora's key useful in this regard. (AMD)

Agaricus sp. (near *albolutescens*)

Caps 6–18 cm broad, convex to plane, smooth or fibrillose (see Glossary), cracking into warts in dry weather, cream to pale yellow when young becoming yellow orange to ochraceous in age, bruising tawny yellow to yellow orange; gills white becoming grayish pink, then dark reddish brown; stalk 6–15 cm long, 2–4 cm thick, enlarged at the base, white staining yellowish; ring thin and membranous, white or yellow stained; odor of anise; spore print chocolate brown.

COMMENTS   This robust species occurs under oaks and conifers and is similar in many respects to *A. silvicola*. It differs in size, in the development of pronounced warts on the cap under dry conditions, and the dark reddish brown gills. In these respects it resembles *A. crocodilinus*, a grassland species reported in eastern New Mexico. (AMD)

Agaricus sp.

Agaricus silvaticus Fries

Caps 4–12 cm broad, covered with small reddish brown to brown scales; flesh turning dull red to reddish brown when exposed or bruised; gills white at first becoming pinkish gray to pink and finally dark reddish brown; stalk 6–11 cm tall, 1–2 cm thick, enlarged at the base, white staining brownish pink to reddish brown; ring thin, membrane white, collapsing and appressed to the stalk. (MNA, MSM)

COMMENTS   A reportedly edible species, it is widely distributed in conifer forests across North America. Caution is recommended in eating it since it is easily confused with the poisonous *A. hondensis*.

Agaricus silvicola (Vitt.) Pk.

Caps 5–14 cm broad, white, smooth to obscurely scaly becoming yellowish at the center and in areas of bruising; gills light pink turning chocolate brown in age; stalk up to 15 cm tall, 1–2.5 cm thick, slightly enlarged at the base, white staining lemon yellow; the attached annulus large, double,

Agaricus silvaticus

Agaricus silvicola

and white staining yellow; spore print chocolate brown; almond odor. (MSM, SWM)

COMMENTS   This species is found scattered to clustered in mixed conifer and deciduous forests of the Canadian and Hudsonian zones as one of the most commonly encountered *Agaricus* species in the Southwest. As one of the yellow-staining species, it is not recommended as edible. Its look-alikes are the meadow-associated *A. arvensis* (LAS, MNA), which is licorice flavored and edible, and *A. xanthodermus*, a poisonous species infrequently encountered in the Southwest except in southern California. (LAS)

Family Strophariaceae

Members of this family have purplish brown to chocolate-brown spore prints. Because of the close similarities between the three genera of the family (*Naematoloma, Psilocybe,* and *Stropharia*) difficulties in classification are great. As has been done by some other authors, species of all three genera are discussed here collectively. (SGM)

Naematolomas have a moist to dry cap, lack an annulus, and are typically found growing in clusters on wood. They resemble Pholiotas to some degree. Psilocybes are small mushrooms with conical to strongly convex caps. They have stalks that are long, thin, with rings, and bruise bluish in species that have hallucinogens. They are typically found on dung. Stropharias are larger mushrooms that occur singly or scattered on grass, buried plant debris, or occasionally on dung. They are similar in appearance to some members of the Agaricaceae. However, the gills are attached to the stalk and the surface of the cap is fibrous rather than fleshy. The stalks have a conspicuous ring when young and the caps are sticky or viscid. Only the Stropharias occur with any regularity in the Southwest, although Psilocybes become more frequent in moist habitats. There are species in all three genera that are known to be poisonous, and others contain hallucinogens. Therefore, the group as a whole is not recommended for eating.

Stropharia kauffmanii Smith

Caps 5–12 cm broad, convex to plane, dry, grayish brown scales over a yellowish ground color; margin with veil remnants; gills attached, crowded, pallid to light grayish brown, thin and relatively fragile; stalk 1–

Stropharia kauffmanii

3 cm thick, equal, with a prominent annulus and a series of squamules attached below the impermanent annulus; spore print purplish black; odor and taste disagreeable. (AMD, SWM)

COMMENTS   This handsome mushroom strongly resembles the small specimens of *Agaricus*. (AMD, BSM, MSM, SWM) It occurs in mixed aspen and conifer stands in the Canadian zone. Fruiting occurs following monsoon rains in summer and fall. *S. riparia* with a pale yellow to olivaceous cap and a thin stalk occurs with aspen and with hardwoods along stream banks of the Riparian zone. (SGM) *S. coronilla*, a more robust look-alike for *S. riparia*, fruits in grassy areas. (LAS, SGM, MNA) *S. semiglobata* with a slimy yellow cap and lilac-brown gills, and *Psilocybe coprophila* with a tacky, brownish cap, brown gills, and yellowish brown stalk, are related species that occur on dung. (LAS, SGM)

Family Cortinariaceae

This family, as one of the largest, is also one of the most difficult in which to identify species. Many are yet undescribed. It contains a large number of poisonous species and because species identification requires microscopic examination, this family is not recommended for eating. For the most part, the genera have distinctively colored spore prints. In *Hebeloma* it is dingy brown, in *Gymnopilus* it is bright rusty orange, in *Inocybe* it is earth brown, in *Pholiota* it is dark brown to gray brown, and in *Cortinarius* it is rusty brown. The veil is a major distinguishing characteristic of *Cortinarius* because of its unique cobweblike appearance (the cortina: see Glossary). Veils may be present or absent in the other genera, but they are typically present in *Cortinarius*. Many of the species of the family are mycorrhizal with conifers. Therefore this family is well represented in the forests of the Southwest.

There are more than six hundred species in *Cortinarius* and nearly all are terrestrial woodland inhabitants. Much taxonomic work remains for the many diverse species found in the Southwest. For this reason, few will be treated in this book. In general, Cortinari are divided into subgenera on the basis of the viscid condition of the cap and stalk, and the basal swelling of the stalk. In *Inocybe*, odor is a distinctive characteristic. Of the more than five hundred species in *Inocybe*, most are small, nondescript mushrooms with a dry, conical cap with a coarsely fibrous surface. *Hebeloma* contains fewer species which are characterized by dull brown, convex caps with a sticky surface, presence or absence of a veil which when present is weakly

Cortinarius glaucopus group

developed and soon disappears, and attached gills with white edges and beaded droplets on the gill surface in young specimens. Like species of *Cortinarius*, Hebelomas are robust and appear temptingly edible, *but none should ever be eaten*. Several are severely poisonous and these species are difficult to identify. Pholiotas typically have conspicuously scaly caps, attached gills, and occur on wood in large clusters. *Gymnopilus* is a wood inhabitant that often occurs in clusters but does not have a conspicuously scaly cap and stalk. The spore print is rusty orange to orange-brown. *Pholiota* is classified in the Strophariaceae by other authors but is placed in this family on the basis of its brown to rusty brown spore print. (LAS, MNA)

Cortinarius glaucopus group

Caps 4–10 cm, convex to plane, smooth, viscid, cinnamon ocher at the center and lighter at the margin with a lilac to olive tint; gills closely spaced, pale lavender to violet in young specimens becoming rusty brown as the spore masses mature; stalk 6–8 cm long, 1–2 cm thick, with a basal bulb; strands of the cortina become rusty brown with trapped spores. (LAS, MNA)

COMMENTS   This is a common species in the conifer forests, particularly spruce and fir of the Hudsonian zone but also in the Canadian zone. It is a widely distributed and variable species.

Cortinarius metarius group

Cap 2–5 cm broad, hemispheric to convex, with a low central knob, yellow to yellow-brown with brown stains; the margin inrolled when young; gills pinkish to pinkish buff, crowded; stalk equal, 3–7 cm long, 3–8 mm thick, white becoming yellowish, with a light zone of yellowish veil tissue in young specimens; spore print rusty brown. (SGM)
COMMENTS   Common in needle litter beneath ponderosa pine in the Transition zone, this species is similar in appearance to the dangerously poisonous, *C. gentilis.* (LAS) *C. cedretorum* is also a yellow-capped species with a basal swelling on the stalk and has been reported to occur in the Southwest. (AMD)

Gymnopilus spectabilis (Fr.) A. H. Smith

Caps 5–18 cm broad, convex to plane, margins often wavy when in contact with adjacent caps; surface smooth in youth and becoming finely scaly in age, bright yellow-orange to deep rusty orange or reddish brown in age; flesh pale yellowish; gills yellow becoming rusty, attached, broad; stalk 8–20 cm long, 1–4 cm thick, thickest in the middle and narrow at the base, solid, firm, often twisted or bent, ring yellow to rusty, membranous or fibrillose forming a distinct line on the stalk; spore print bright rusty orange. (LAS, MSM)
COMMENTS   A truly spectacular mushroom in size and color, *G. spectabilis* occurs on both hardwoods and conifers. It is especially common on stumps of ponderosa pine in the Transition zone. The smaller *G. sapineus* is also common on rotting logs and humus of pine. Both have a strong bitter taste that renders them inedible.

Hebeloma crustuliniforme (St. Amans) Quellet

Caps 3–10 cm broad, broadly convex, with a brownish central knob, otherwise cream-colored to light tan, viscid; the margin inrolled at first, then expanded and wavy; gills white to dull brown, margins whitish with

Cortinarius metarius group

Gymnopilus spectabilis

Hebeloma crustuliniforme

Hebeloma insigne

beaded droplets; stalk equal to a bulbous base, white, smooth, veil absent; spore print brown; odor radishlike. (LAS, MNA, MSM, SWM)

COMMENTS   This attractive, robust mushroom is mycorrhizal with conifers and is found in clusters and arcs in the Transition and Canadian zones. It is definitely poisonous as are most members of the genus.

Hebeloma insigne Smith

Caps 5–10 cm broad, broadly convex becoming flat, viscid but quickly drying, pinkish brown to cinnamon-brown in the center, lighter toward the margin; gills broad, notched at site of attachment with stalk, pale clay-colored when young becoming pinkish gray and finally pallid brown at maturity, spotted at the margins from beaded droplets; stalk 6–8 cm long, 1–3 cm thick and equal along length, whitish surface with concentric zones of pallid scales, bulbous at base when young.

COMMENTS   Found under conifers this species is similar to the poisonous *Hebeloma sinapizans* as described by American authors. (SWM) It lacks the radishlike taste of that species but its edibility is unknown.

Inocybe geophylla var. *lilacina* (Pk.) Boudier

Cap 1–3 cm broad, conical to convex with a central knob, whitish gray becoming grayish lilac to pinkish lilac in age; stalk 1–3 mm thick, slightly swollen at the base; gills attached, whitish, becoming colored as the cap; spore print brown; odor spermatic. (BSM, LAS)

COMMENTS   Two names have been used to describe this species; one for the uncolored form, *I. geophylla*, and one for the lilac-colored form, *I. lilacina*. Since both occur together in coniferous and hardwood stands, it is reasonable to consider them as the same species. All forms of this mushroom are considered poisonous.

There are many species of *Inocybe* in southwestern conifer forests. All are small- to medium-sized mushrooms and most are mycorrhizal. They are typically terrestrial and the fruiting bodies have conical caps with fibrillose or scaly surfaces.

Inocybe geophylla var. lilacina

Pholiota squarrosa

Pholiota squarrosa (Fr.) Kummer

Cap and stalk covered with coarse upturned scales; scales yellowish brown over an ochraceous background; cap 3–10 cm broad, dry, hemispheric when young becoming broadly convex; portions of veil tissue clinging to the cap margin; gills attached, crowded, pale yellow or greenish yellow becoming dull rusty brown as the spores mature; stalk 4–10 cm long, 4–12 mm thick, with an inconspicuous membranous ring; odor and taste of garlic. (AMD, LAS, MNA)

COMMENTS   As brown-spored mushrooms, Pholiotas characteristically grow in clusters on wood and possess tacky to viscid caps and veil remnants often as a ring on the stalk. *Pholiota squarrosa* is a very distinctive species that grows at the base of dead or dying hardwoods, particularly aspen, and occasionally conifers. Caution is recommended when eating any Pholiota. This particular species has caused severe gastric upset in some people, including myself, while others have had no reaction to it at all. It has a very appealing garliclike flavor that makes it a favorite of the Basque sheepherders in our area. Fruiting is abundant even in dry years when other mushrooms fail to appear.

Pholiota terrestris

Pholiota terrestris Overholts

Caps 2–10 cm broad, hemispheric at first then convex to nearly plane, brown, covered with downcurved brown scales, a gelatinous layer below the scales; gills attached, crowded, pinkish gray to dull brown; stalk 2–8 cm long, 5–10 mm thick, white staining brownish at the base, covered with scales similar to those of the cap; spore print brown. (LAS, MNA, MSM)

COMMENTS   The densely scaly fruiting bodies of this species emerge in grassy areas and along roadways presumably from buried wood. Smith reports it to be edible but not highly rated. (SGM) Another species common in mixed conifer-hardwood forests at mid elevations is *P. albocrenulata*. It has a distinctive red-brown cap and grayish gills with whitish edges. (MNA)

Family Pluteaceae and Family Entolomataceae

These two families represent the pink-spored mushrooms, those which produce flesh-colored, pink, or sordid pink hues in the spore print. Some members of the Tricholomataceae have much less intense, pale pinkish spores. *Entoloma*, *Leptonia*, and *Nolanea*, among other genera in the Entolomataceae (Rhodophyllaceae) typically have fruiting bodies with attached gills, stalks that are generally inseparable from the cap, and distinctly angular spores. By contrast, *Pluteus* and *Volvariella* of the Pluteaceae (Volvariaceae) have free gills and nonangular spores. *Volvariella* has a conspicuous volva. The species of the Entolomataceae, which may be numerous on occasion in the Southwest, are associated with conifer forests but they are generally too small to be considered for eating. Because of the difficulty in identifying most species, even with the use of microscopic features and because several species are poisonous, especially the larger Entolomas, the entire family should be avoided.

   Pluteus and *Volvariella* species are as a group generally considered to be edible. They occur, however, in low numbers and are not particularly robust; edibility is unknown or questionable for many of them. Until the taxonomic difficulties have been resolved, the pink-spored mushrooms will receive little attention in mushroom guides.

Pluteus lutescens (Fr.) Bresdola

Caps 2–5 cm broad, brown to olive-brown, flat to slightly depressed at the center; surface dry, smooth to minutely scaly at the center; gills broad and crowded, cream to yellow becoming pinkish as the spores mature, free

Pluteus lutescens

from the stalk; stalk bright yellow, uniform width and slender; spore print flesh-colored to pink. (AMD)

COMMENTS   As one of the more attractive members of the genus, *P. lutescens* is found singly or in small clusters on decaying wood of both deciduous and coniferous trees. Another member, *P. atromarginatus*, is often found on the cut ends of conifer stumps. It has white gills with conspicuous black margins. (LAS) The pink gilled *P. cervinus* is common on aspen, oak, and occasionally on conifers. (LAS)

APHYLLOPHORALES-CANTHARELLOID, CORAL, TOOTHED, CRUST AND WOODY-PORED FUNGI

This large assemblage of diverse Basidiomycete fungi is grouped together on the basis of one or both of the following characteristics: (1) the exposed hymenophore, the structure bearing the fertile tissue, is nongilled (hence the name Aphyllophorales), and (2) the fruiting body is generally woody, leathery, or coarsely fleshy, often growing as a perennial or long-lasting as an annual. Only a few of the many hundreds of species are included in this guide. Most are cosmopolitan in distribution and occur as saprophytes on wood. Only a very few are fleshy enough to be edible. Another large group of nongilled fungi is the Gasteromycetes whose fertile tissue is enclosed within the fruiting body tissue. These "stomach fungi" are discussed in a separate section.

The Cantharellaceae is a family of mushrooms commonly referred to as chanterelles. The fertile gill-like ridges are typically blunt or rounded in cross section. There is often little distinction in the tissue of the cap and stalk, both appearing continuous with one another. Most species are highly prized edibles. They are widespread throughout coniferous forests and also to some degree in mixed conifer-hardwood stands. Often appearing in the same place year after year, their location is kept a jealously guarded secret. Only the yellow chanterelle, *Cantharellus cibarius*, and the scaly chanterelles, *Gomphus floccosus* and *G. kauffmanii*, occur with any frequency in the Southwest. The latter two are unpalatable and not recommended for eating.

Toothlike spines on the lower surfaces of the fruiting body are characteristic of the Hydnaceae. The texture of these mushrooms ranges from the tough and woody *Hydnellum* species, to the fleshy and agariclike *Hydnum* and *Dentinum* species. Most of the Hydnaceae are stalked but some are attached directly to wood substrates (as in Hericium). In some classifications the genus *Sarcodon* is presented for Hydnums with a brown spore deposit and the substitution of *Hydnum* for the genus *Dentinum*, which has a white spore deposit.

The fruiting bodies of the coral fungi range from small, erect club-shaped stalks to large, complex leaflike or corallike masses.

The polypore fungi are by far the most numerous and diverse of the nongilled mushrooms. The woody united tubes may be borne on fruiting bodies similar to those of the fleshy boletes, but the stalks are not usually centrally attached to the cap and the tissues are generally tough and woody. In most cases there is no stalk at all; the caps are attached directly to wood. Polypores are collectively referred to as wood-decay fungi for that is the functional role of most of the species included here. Their fruiting bodies are found on dead logs, stumps, and other plant debris, or they are associated with living trees and shrubs as parasites.

A large number of wood decay fungi in the Southwest have only minute pores or no pores at all. These are the Crust fungi whose fruiting bodies are inconspicuously positioned on the lower surfaces of downed wood. Their hymenophore is flattened and exposed. These fungi are well adapted to the severe environmental conditions of the southwestern deserts. As members of several families, including the Corticiaceae, Stereaceae, and the Thelephoraceae, they comprise the majority of the macroscopic fungi in hot deserts. The reader is directed to the excellent keys of Gilbertson and Ryvarden (1986) for their classification and identification. Descriptions of the commonly occurring species are presented in alphabetical order.

Key to the Cantharelloid, Coral, Toothed, and Woody-pored Aphyllophorales

1a. Fruiting body with cap and stalk; cap with blunt, thick ridges or plates that descend the stalk; ridges often wrinkled and interconnected with cross veins 2

1b. Not as above 3

    2a. Cap surface smooth . . . . . (p. 125) *Cantharellus cibarius*

    2b. Cap surface scaly . . . .
    . . . (pp. 132, 135) *Gomphus floccosus* and *G. kauffmanii*

3a. Fruiting body a cluster of multibranched, coralloid structures or single club-shaped stalks 4

3b. Not as above 10

    4a. Fruiting body with coralloid branches terminating in an expanded crownlike apex   (p. 126) *Clavicorona pyxidata*

    4b. Not as above 5

5a. Fruiting body as single club-shaped stalks . . . .
. . . . (p. 126) *Clavariadelphus borealis*

5b. Not as above 5

    6a. Fruiting body sparingly branched, white with minutely pointed tips . . . . (p. 129) *Clavulina cristata*

    6b. Not as above 7

7a. Fruiting body unbranched but in clusters, cylindric to flattened near the tip . . . . (p. 126) *Clavaria purpurea*

7b. Not as above 8

    8a. Fruiting body a dense cluster of wavy, platelike branches resembling a head of lettuce . . . . (p. 142) *Sparassis crispa*

    8b. Not as above 9

9a. Fruiting body densely branched; branches bright yellow; on wood
. . . . (p. 141) *Ramaria rasilispora* group

9b. As above but branches ochraceous to brown, taste bitter; on
ground . . . . (p. 141) *Ramaria formosa*

10a. Fruiting body with spines (teeth) 11

10b. Not as above 13

11a. Fruiting body with cap and stalk; tissues fibrous and tough . . . . .
. . . . (p. 135) *Hydnellum scrobiculatum* group

11b. Fruiting body without a stalk; tissues fleshy 12

12a. Fruiting body a solid mass of tissue with pendant spines
over the surface . . . . (p. 135) *Hericium erinaceum*

12b. Fruiting body stalked, cap with scales, spore print brown
. . . . (p. 136) *Hydnum imbricatum*

13a. Fruiting body lacking a stalk; cap with leathery gills . . . .
. . . . (p. 132) *Gloeophyllum sepiarium*

13b. Not as above 14

14a. Stalk absent; cap pored, thick, woody, and perennial . . 15

14b. As above but cap more or less fleshy or pliable when fresh
and annual 17

15a. Cap small, hoof-shaped, on branch scars of standing trees . . . . . .
. . . . (p. 138) *Phellinus tremulae*

15b. Cap large, thick, and shelflike 16

16a. Cap deeply zoned with a brownish red margin covered with
a sticky or crusty varnish . . . . (p. 130) *Fomitopsis pinicola*

16b. Cap without large distinct zones, colored gray-brown to
dull reddish brown; the surface hard and brittle in age with
conspicuous cracks . . . . (p. 130) *Ganoderma applanatum*

17a. Fruiting body large compound, typically with many rusty brown
caps from a common base, cap surface woolly, cap margins
ochraceous to orange when young . . (p. 136) *Phaeolus schweinitzii*

17b. Not as above 18

18a. Cap and pores orange to dull reddish orange fading to
white or cream; pores large, unequal and torn, hanging as
ragged strands . . . . . . (p. 138) *Pycnoporellus alboluteus*

18b. Caps clustered in tiers on wood, distinctly zoned; zones
multicolored, ranging from blackish brown, gray-blue, yellow, and occasionally pink . . (p. 129) *Coriolus versicolor*

Cantharellus cibarius

Cantharellus cibarius Fries

Fruiting body short, robust, bright yellow to yellow-orange with a funnel-shaped cap; cap 2–6 cm broad with a wavy uneven margin; gills as blunt ridges, decurrent, cross veins occasional between ridges; stalk continuous with the cap, thick above and tapering toward the base, uneven in cross section, colored like the cap or somewhat lighter; odor pleasant and fruity; spore print pale yellow. (AMD, BSM, LAS, MNA, MSM, SWM)

COMMENTS   This species is one of the most common and widely distributed of the chanterelles. It can be found in summer and fall fruiting under pine and mixed conifer stands of the Transition and Canadian zones. In some varieties the gill-like ridges are more pronounced. They resemble in this form a look-alike, *Hygrophoropsis aurantiaca*, which is questionably edible. This false chanterelle is easily distinguished by its distinctively forked, thin-edged gills and lack of the fruity odor. The stature of the southwestern variety is much reduced in comparison to those in other regions and the riblike gills typically have prominent cross veins.

Clavaria purpurea Fries

Fruiting bodies in clusters, fleshy and fragile; cylindrical to spindle-shaped, erect and unbranched, 2.5–10 cm tall, 2–6 mm thick; grayish purple to deep purple, fading vinaceous buff in age; tips tapered, acute or blunt. (AMD, LAS, MSM)

COMMENTS   The purple coloration is distinctive for this species, which fruits under spruce and fir in the Canadian and Hudsonian zone. The pure white *C. vermicularis* is common under hardwoods, particularly oak but is cosmopolitan and abundant in wet years. (BSM, MNA)

Clavariadelphus borealis Wells and Kempton

Fruiting body yellow to orange, unbranched, erect, 5–12 cm tall, club-shaped, narrow at the base and expanded at the apex; apex rounded or truncate, puckered around the margin; stalk darkens to reddish orange and becomes flushed with lilac pigment in some specimens; spore print white. (SWM)

COMMENTS   This conspicuous coral fungus occurs in association with pines and occasionally with other conifers in the Transition and Canadian zones. It has a bitter flavor whereas its look-alike, *C. truncatus*, is mildly sweet and produces an orange spore print. Fruiting bodies of both have truncated apices. (AMD, BSM, MNA, MSM) Other similar fungi encountered in southwestern forests include: *C. pistillaris*, common in deciduous forests (MNA); *C. ligula*, a thin yellow species in conifer duff (AMD, LAS, MNA); and a tongue-shaped sac fungus, *Spathularia flavida*. (LAS, MNA)

Clavicorona pyxidata (Fr.) Doty

Fruiting body a thick cluster of slender, evenly branched stalks; branches arising at different levels, pinkish to light tan, narrow at the base and terminating in an expanded crownlike apex with light-colored, toothlike projections; spore print white; taste acrid to peppery. (LAS, MNA)

COMMENTS   The branches of this coral fungus resemble the parapets of a castle and the minutely toothed apices resemble the points of a crown, hence its generic name. It is common on dead wood of aspen and occasionally willows, fruiting in summer and early fall. It is reportedly edible. A look-alike is *Ramaria stricta* which also occurs on aspen, but it lacks the

Clavaria purpurea

Clavariadelphus borealis

Clavicorona pyxidata

Clavulina cristata

crownlike tips on the ultimate branches. Neither are particularly good to eat. Their consistency and flavor are poor. (LAS)

Clavulina cristata (Fr.) Schroeter

Fruiting bodies 2–6 cm tall, white to yellowish cream-colored, in clusters of irregularly flattened branches, typically with small toothlike projections at the branch apices; spore print white. (AMD, LAS, MNA, MSM)
COMMENTS   Large groups of this coral fungus appear as fairy rings or scattered circular clusters on conifer litter, especially under pines in the Transition zone following the monsoon rains. Edibility is reportedly fair.

Coriolus versicolor (Fr.) Quellet

Fruiting bodies usually as an overlapping series of thin semicircular caps; cap 2.5–10 cm wide, often fused laterally, flat to wavy; surface silky to velvety with prominent multicolored zones, typically in tones of brown, reddish brown, bluish, blackish or yellow, the outermost zone light yellow or ocher; pore surface white to yellowish. (AMD, BSM, LAS, MNA)

Coriolus versicolor

COMMENTS   Called "Turkey Tail," this wood-decay fungus is found on dead wood or wounds of deciduous trees in the Riparian zone and oak forests. It is also known as *Trametes* and *Polyporus versicolor*. Two other common wood-decay fungi with fruiting bodies arranged in overlapping tiers on logs or stumps are *Trichaptum* (*Hirschioporus*) *abietinum*, associated with subalpine fir (LAS, SNGM) and *Bjerkjandra* (*Polyporus*) *adusta*, associated with hardwoods, particularly aspen. (LAS, SNGM)

Fomitopsis pinicola (Fr.) Karsten

Fruiting body up to 30 cm or more in diameter, with conspicuous furrowed growth zones, tapering from a thick basal attachment on wood to a narrow rounded margin; pores small, angular, cream-colored, produced in concentric layers; the layers cream-colored to light brown; spore deposit is barely visible. (AMD, LAS)

COMMENTS   Also known as *Fomes pinicola*, this common bracket fungus is associated with coniferous trees, particularly pine. Attached to aging standing trees, snags, and wood stumps, it is readily recognized by its thick-zoned cap with a crusted reddish resinous zone near the margin. Its woody tissue is palatable only to fungus beetles.

Ganoderma applanatum (Pers.) Pat.

Fruiting body up to 60 cm broad as a thick fan-shaped bracket; perennial growth marked by ridged zones on the upper surface; upper surface hard, hornlike and cracked, pale gray to grayish brown or brown; flesh yellowish brown or cinnamon brown; tube layers white or whitish when fresh and staining brown when scratched; tube layers separated by chocolate brown tissue that also fills the tubes; spore print reddish brown. (LAS, MNA)

COMMENTS   This species is called the "Artist's Conk" because the white pore surface turns brown when scratched. It is primarily associated with decay of hardwoods, particularly aspen in the Canadian zone but it also decays a variety of conifers. The smaller *Fomitopsis subrosea* has a pinkish to brownish pink pore surface and is found on dead wood, usually conifers. (LAS)

Fomitopsis pinicola

Ganoderma applanatum

Gloeophyllum sepiarium (Wulf. ex Fr.) Karsten

Fruiting body a stalkless, semicircular bracket attached to cracks or cut ends of dead conifer wood; cap with distinct zones, hairy to nearly smooth, the innermost zones rust brown, the outermost zone bright yellow to orange when fresh; hymenophore as gill-like plates sometimes with cross connections forming irregular wide-mouth pores, cream to yellowish, brown in age; spore print cream-colored. (LAS)

COMMENTS   This is one of the most abundant and widespread of the wood-decay fungi. It causes a "brown rot" of conifer and is especially common on downed trees in areas of timber harvest. Because of its tolerance to drought, it can also decay building timber and railroad ties.

Gomphus floccosus (Schw.) Singer

Fruiting body trumpet-shaped, large and robust; cap up to 15 cm broad, covered with coarse, erect, orange-yellow to reddish orange scales; gills as fertile wrinkled ridges, white to cream-colored, descending the stalk; stalk not distinct from the cap, fibrous, hollow; spore print ochraceous. (AMD, LAS, MNA, MSM)

COMMENTS   This chanterellelike mushroom fruits in the fall in the Canadian zone associated with Douglas fir and limber pine. Some who have eaten it have reported gastrointestinal irritation. Its fibrous flesh makes it unappealing in any event.

Gloeophyllum sepiarium

Gomphus floccosus

Gomphus kauffmanii

Hericium erinaceum

Gomphus kauffmanii (Smith) Singer

Caps 10–40 cm broad, funnel-shaped, and continuous with the stalk, clay color to ochraceous tawny, covered with large recurved brittle scales, margin uneven; underside (fertile hymenophore) with deep veins or ridges descending the stalk, sometimes poroid near the top, yellow when young becoming pallid to pinkish buff in age; stalk 8–15 cm long and tapered to the base. (SNGM)

COMMENTS   Found scattered or in clusters (not fused together) under conifers in the Canadian and Hudsonian zones. Edibility is unknown but caution is advised since some people have had problems upon eating *G. floccosus*.

Hericium erinaceum Persoon

Fruiting body without a distinct cap, arising as a mound of tissue covered with pendant spines; spines up to 5 cm long, soft and pliant when fresh, white becoming yellow-brown to dingy brown in age; spore print white. (LAS)

COMMENTS   Called the "Hedgehog" fungus or "Bear's Head" fungus, this edible species typically grows on standing and downed oaks although it is found on other hardwoods of the Riparian zone. Two very different appearing corallike white Hericiums, *H. ramosum* (on aspen) (AMD, LAS) and *H. abietis* (on conifers) (AMD, MSM) are also edible when young.

Hydnellum scrobiculatum group

Fruiting bodies tough and fibrous even when fresh, cinnamon to dark reddish brown; cap 6–10 cm broad, continued growth of the margins often resulting in several fused caps; stalk 2–5 cm long and 2–3 cm thick with a rootlike base; spines beneath the cap 1–4 mm long, brown at the base with light tips; stalk 2–4 cm long with a tuberous base; spore print rusty brown. (SNGM)

COMMENTS   Several varieties of *Hydnellum* occur in southwestern coniferous forests, all of which are difficult to identify without microscopic characteristics. Most are too tough and bitter-tasting to be considered edible. (AMD, LAS)

Hydnum imbricatum Fries

Caps 6–20 cm broad, depressed at the center; surface dry, light brown with large, coarse, dark brown scales that are upturned in age, finally dark brown overall; flesh white to brownish, soft, teeth (spines) pale brown becoming darker; stalk colored like the cap, enlarging downward toward the base; spore print brown. (AMD, LAS, MNA, MSM)

COMMENTS   It fruits abundantly in the Hudsonian zone in association with spruce and fir. It is reported to occur also with hardwoods. The bitter taste makes it a poor edible. *H. ramosum* with its conspicuously cracked irregular cap occurs with pine and other conifers.

Phaeolus schweinitzii (Fr.) Pat.

Fruiting body attached to wood with one to several fused caps arising from a common fleshy base; caps highly variable in size, 4–20 cm broad, shell-shaped or united laterally or elongate; margin wavy, colored yellow-orange to deep reddish orange when young; upper surface densely hairy becoming smooth in age, dark brown; flesh yellowish, tough, and fibrous; pores

Hydnellum scrobiculatum group

Hydnum imbricatum

Phaeolus schweinitzii

mustard yellow to greenish yellow, bruising dark brown or black; spore print cream to light yellow. (LAS)

COMMENTS   Also known as *Polyporus schweinitzii*, this species causes a serious heart rot in conifers. It is especially abundant in ponderosa pine and Douglas fir in the Transition and Canadian zones. The size of its fruiting body is much smaller in the Southwest than elsewhere. Although inedible, this species is useful as a dye source.

Phellinus tremulae (Bond) Bond and Boriss

Perennial fruiting body an ungulate (hoof-shaped) conk with concentrically furrowed growth zones; zones finely hairy in youth to conspicuously cracked and ragged in age; surface color brown to grayish black or black, often covered with lichen colonies in moist environments; pore surface brown to grayish brown, the small tubes often stuffed with white mycelium following a period of growth; spore print white to cream-colored. (LAS)

COMMENTS   The fruiting bodies characteristically emerge from branch scars (knots) on stems of aspen and other deciduous trees. This fungus can be found in nearly every aspen grove in the western U.S. Large areas of mature aspen in the Southwest show severe wind damage because of heartwood decay caused by this fungus.

Pycnoporellus alboluteus (Ell. and Ev.) Kotl. and Pouz.

Fruiting body spreading on the surface of conifer logs; cap narrow, 1–3 cm, or absent; tissue bright to rusty orange fading to white, spongy in consistency, feltlike when dry, holding water in moist conditions; tubes large with irregular pore openings, with the side walls often torn and ragged; spore print white. (LAS)

COMMENTS   This brightly colored wood-decay fungus can be found in abundance on the lower surfaces of downed fir and spruce logs in the early spring at the edge of melting snowbanks. Another orange-colored fungus on conifer and deciduous trees is *Pycnoporellus cinnabarinus*. It has a shelflike cap, small even pores, and occurs on both conifer and hardwoods in the Riparian zone. (LAS)

Phellinus tremulae

Pycnoporellus alboluteus

Ramaria formosa

Ramaria formosa group

Fruiting body 10–18 cm tall, 2.5–15 cm wide, much branched from a fleshy basal stalk; branches mostly erect, pinkish orange to salmon-colored but fading to dull yellowish or tan in age; tips yellow becoming colored as the branches; stalk fleshy to fibrous, whitish becoming pinkish salmon; taste bitter and biting to the throat when swallowed. (LAS)

COMMENTS   This is a Ramaria to be avoided. It is said to have strong cathartic properties. It fruits primarily under conifers of the Canadian and Hudsonian zones but it also occurs with hardwoods of the Riparian zone.

Ramaria rasilispora group

Fruiting body on dead wood arising as numerous densely crowded branches from one to several fleshy stalks, 5–15 cm tall; branches progressively smaller towards the apex, light yellow to lemon yellow; stalks white near their attachment on wood, flesh somewhat brittle, not changing color when bruised; spore print pale yellow. (MNA)

Ramaria rasilispora

COMMENTS   This brightly colored coral fungus fruits on well-rotted wood of conifers particularly spruce and fir. It approximates the description of *R. flava* of European distribution. Miller (MNA) reports these yellow Ramarias to be edible but caution is recommended. *R. sanguinea* has yellow branches with tips and flesh that bruise vinaceous reddish brown. *R. rasilispora* has been reported to occur in the forests of the Sierra Nevada and Cascades in the spring. (AMD, MSM)

Sparassis crispa Wulf. ex Fr.

Fruiting body appearing as a large lettucelike cluster of white to pale yellow leaflike branches; the branch margins flattened and expanded, wavy; torn flesh white below the yellow-brown surface with central rootlike basal attachment; spore print white. (AMD, BSM, LAS, MNA, MSM)
COMMENTS   A widespread but not common coral fungus, *S. crispa*, also known as *S. radicata*, is considered one of the choice edibles of the Southwest. Easily recognized by its cauliflowerlike appearance, it fruits in the fall under a variety of conifers and is a probable parasite on their roots.

JELLY FUNGI: TREMELLALES AND AURICULARIALES

A number of Basidiomycetes have totally gelatinous fruiting bodies. Many are brightly colored and conspicuous on wet logs and dead plant debris but disappear during dry periods. One of the brown to black-colored species, *Auricularia auricula*, has a large wrinkled fruiting body whose shape occasionally resembles a human ear. Along with *A. mesenterica*, this species is a popular edible and can be readily cultured on conifer wood in a temperate to cool environment.

Auricularia auricula (Hook) Under.

Fruiting body cuplike to ear-shaped, brown to blackish brown, tough and gelatinous, attached centrally or laterally; flaring outward with several conspicuous ribs or veins exiting down to the point of attachment; flesh thin and rubbery, the inner surface covered with a film of white spores, drying to thin black, horny, wrinkled scales. (BSM, LAS, MSM, SWM)
COMMENTS   Found in clusters on dead conifer wood, particularly fir, in the Canadian and Hudsonian zones this fungus is a major condiment in

Sparassis crispa

Auricularia auricula

Dacrymyces palmatus

Gueopiniopsis alpinus

oriental cooking and therefore cultured extensively especially in China. It can be purchased in the vegetable sections of large supermarkets under the name of "wood ear" along with the common table mushroom, *Agaricus brunnescens.*

Dacrymyces palmatus (Schw.) Bres.

Fruiting body a bright orange-yellow to orange mass of lobed, convoluted gelatinous tissue, lobes with definite boundaries firm when young and whitish at the point of attachment; spore print white to pale yellow. (BSM, LAS, MNA, MSM)

COMMENTS   This species is abundant on wet conifer logs and stumps in high-elevation life zones. Its taste is unpleasant. *Tremella mesenterica* (LAS) is similar in appearance but remains firm throughout development, yellow to yellow-orange and grows on wood of deciduous trees. Another species of jelly fungus, *Pseudohydnum gelatinosum,* has an erect stalked fruiting body which is tonguelike with short spines on the lower surface. The flesh is gelatinous and white over the toothed area and is colored pink to pinkish purple on the upper surface. (LAS, MNA, MSM) A look-alike is *Phlogiotis helvelloides,* a jelly fungus not reported as yet in the region but is reported from southern California. (LAS, MSM)

Gueopiniopsis alpinus (Tracy and Earle) Bres.

Fruiting body small, cup-shaped, and filled with gel, mostly less than 1 cm; bright yellow to orange, with the narrow, tapered base attached to dead logs and twigs, appearing as minute, dull orange scales on wood when dry; spore print pale yellow. (LAS, MNA)

COMMENTS   This species is widespread and abundant in the coniferous forest of the Canadian and Hudsonian zones. It can be readily found on wet wood at the edges of melting snowbanks in spring and summer. Its small size and flavor do little to recommend it as an edible.

Stomach Fungi

PUFFBALLS AND ALLIES AND AGARICOID GASTEROMYCETES

If one were to designate a group of mushrooms as characteristic of the deserts and dry sites of the Southwest, it would clearly be the class Gasteromycetes. The class embraces a broad range of fungal forms to include puffballs, stalked puffballs, earthstars, bird's nests, stinkhorns, and the Agaricoid Gasteromycetes. The fruiting bodies of puffballs and their allies are all similar in that the spore-bearing surface, the gleba, is enclosed by one or more layers of protective tissue, the peridium. The prefix *gastro-*, or stomach, is therefore quite appropriate for the general name of the group. The variety of shapes of the fruiting bodies is but a reflection of the different ways in which the spore mass is developed and dispersed for reproduction.

The peridium is an important feature of puffballs in that it provides protection for the developing spores until they are mature and can be released. The protection is needed in the harsh and sometimes severe environment of deserts and dry forest sites where many of the true and false puffballs are found. The stalked species commonly occur in sandy soils where the elevation of the spore mass above the drifting sand insures effective dispersal by wind. The fleshy members of the Gasteromycetes, the stinkhorns, are found in moist sites, and their spore masses are wet instead of dry. They are dispersed by insects rather than by wind.

The Agaricoid Gasteromycetes represent a transitional fungus form, that between a stalked, gilled mushroom and a puffball form with a peridium. They are also similar to false truffles in that the primordium is often hypogeous at first but the development of the stalk or *stalk-columella* (see Glossary) clearly shows their relationship to Agarics. The gills, or in some cases pores, are evident within the peridium, but the spores cannot be forcibly discharged as they are in the gilled and pored mushrooms. The greatest diversity and abundance of this mushroom type is found in the West and Southwest, particularly the warm, dry sites of forests and deserts.

Many Gasteromycetes produce fruiting bodies from a hypogeous primordium. As the fruiting body develops it emerges from the soil and plant litter. The Gasteromycetes that remain submerged in soil and litter are known as "false truffles" and are treated under the heading Tuberlike Basidiomycetes.

The true puffballs as opposed to the hard-skinned puffballs (*Scleroderma*) are edible. Because they can be found almost any time and in places where few other kinds of fungi are found, they are quite popular with the avid mycophagist. Young specimens, those without coloration of the cut gleba, are best for eating. The primordia of various mushrooms, such as the poisonous *Amanita*, superficially resemble puffballs. To avoid regrettable mistakes, the presumptive puffball should be sliced lengthwise to reveal the homogeneous white, solid tissue of the gleba. Anything less should be discarded. Immature false truffles resemble puffballs in cross section, but they are hypogeous and lack a powdery spore mass at maturity. Unfortunately, puffballs do not respond well to various methods of freezing or canning. Therefore, they must be quickly consumed as they become available.

There are so many kinds of Gasteromycetes in the Southwest that only a treatment in a volume of their own can possibly do them justice. Representatives of the major groups have been chosen for illustration and discussion. Species descriptions are preceded by a description of the group to which they belong.

Key to Selected Gasteromycetes

1a. Fruiting body sessile and often hypogeous, stalk-columella extending partly into the gleba; gleba remaining enclosed by a thick walled peridium (skin) at maturity (young primordia of stalked puffballs have a similar appearance) . . (p. 151) *Radiigera atrogleba*
1b. Fruiting body not as above 2
    2a. Fruiting bodies superficially resembling gilled mushrooms; sporecase or caps with deformed gills or cavities which may or may not be exposed at maturity; stalks tall or

short usually extending through the gleba to the top of the fruiting body; spores not forcibly discharged (Agaricoid Gasteromycetes) 3

2b. Not as above 7

3a. Fruiting body with a short, poorly developed stalk 4

3b. Fruiting body with a well-developed stalk 5

4a. Fruiting body resembling a *Chroogomphus* gilled mush-room, cap dull orange staining vinaceous; glebal plates yellow-orange becoming dark gray . . . .
. . . . (p. 151) *Brauniellula nancyae*

4b. Fruiting body resembling an *Agaricus* gilled mushroom; glebal plates brown to black   (p. 151) *Endoptychum* spp.

5a. Fruiting body resembling the gilled mushroom *Coprinus*; mature gleba dark brown to black, powdery, and enclosed at maturity . . .
. . . . (p. 155) *Podaxis pistillaris*

5b. Not as above 6

6a. Fruiting body with exposed gleba of black gill-like plates elevated on a fibrous, woody stalk . . . .
. . . . (p. 155) *Montagnea arenarius*

6b. Fruiting body with gleba enclosed by the peridium until maturity; stalk woody and extending as a columella into the glebal chamber; peridium rupturing at the base of the spore case leaving a ring on the stalk . . . .
. . . . (p. 152) *Longula texensis*

7a. Fruiting body with a recognizable to well-developed stalk 8

7b. Fruiting body lacking a stalk 10

8a. Stalk fleshy; spore mass slimy and foul-smelling . . . .
. . . . (p. 156) *Phallus impudicus*

8b. Stalk fibrous to woody; spore mass powdery 9

9a. Stalk tall, 15–40 cm with a terminal puffball-shaped spore case; peridium firm . . . . (p. 156) *Battarrea phalloides*

9b. Stalk short, usually less than 15 cm tall; peridium usually papery to brittle, opening by an apical pore . . (p. 156) *Tulostoma* and Allies

10a. Fruiting body a small funnel-shaped cup containing one or more small egglike peridioles 11

10b. Fruiting body saclike (puffball shaped) 12

11a. Peridioles attached to the cup wall by a cord, mostly on plant debris and dung . . . . (p. 161) *Cyathus striatus*

11b. Peridioles free within a small thick-walled cup; always on wood . .
. . . . (p. 160) *Crucibulum laeve*

 12a. Immature gleba firm and deeply colored; peridium wall
 also firm to brittle . . . . (pp. 161, 162)
     Scleroderma hypogaeum and *S. michiganense*

 12b. Immature gleba soft and white; peridium wall papery (except in *Astreus* below) 13

13a. Peridium wall double, the outer wall splitting away into starlike
rays 14

13b. Peridium wall not splitting into starlike rays 15

 14a. Outer peridial wall tough to woody, splitting into 7–15
 pointed rays that open when wet and close over the inner
 peridium when dry . . . . . (p. 164) *Astreus hygrometricus*

 14b. Outer peridial wall at first fleshy becoming firm but not
 woody; splitting into from 3 to 10 fleshy rays; recurving
 beneath the inner peridium when wet or remaining expanded; rays membranous when dry . . . .
 . . . . (pp. 164, 167) *Geastrum* spp.

15a. Peridium opening by an apical pore . . . . (p. 167) *Lycoperdon* spp.

15b. Not as above 16

 16a. Fruiting body with a sterile base or pseudostem; up to 25
 cm broad . . . . (p. 167) *Calbovista subsculpta*

 16b. Fruiting body large, up to 50 cm broad, lacking
 pseudostem; peridium breaking up into brownish pyramidal warts at maturity . . . . . . (p. 168) *Calvatia booniana*

Radiigera atrogleba

Brauniellula nancyae

Radiigera atrogleba Zeller

Fruiting body round, 3–5 cm broad, partly hypogeous at maturity, embedded in a mass of mycelium; peridium 2–5 mm thick, white, then strongly pink to vinaceous; gleba of platelike strands radiating out from a knob-shaped sterile basal columella; plates pink at first, then blackish brown. (AMD, SNGM)

COMMENTS This most unusual Gasteromycete appears after periods of moisture in dry sites of coniferous forests, especially under pine in the Transition zone. The fruiting body strongly resembles the egg-shaped primordium of stalked puffballs and stinkhorns. It can be easily distinguished from them on the basis of the knoblike columella with radiating plates.

Brauniellula nancyae Smith

Fruiting body with cap and stalk; cap 1–5 cm broad, convex or depressed; surface dry, ocher to pale orange below a layer of grayish to brownish gray fibrils that become reddish vinaceous in age; cap margin lobed, attached at first to the stalk by thin ochraceous to vinaceous veil; later separating to expose the ochraceous to dark gray spore-bearing plates; stalk extending from the top through the spore mass 3–15 mm long, 8–10 mm thick, ochraceous, orange with deep vinaceous stains in age. (SNGM)

COMMENTS Apart from the platelike gleba which remains enclosed for the most part by the cap, this fungus is remarkably similar to *Chroogomphus vinicolor*. It is restricted in distribution to conifers, especially two- and three-needle pine. Edibility is unknown but it is highly favored by squirrels.

Endoptychum depressum Singer and Smith

Fruiting body with cap and stalk; cap 3–10 cm broad, rounded with center depressed at maturity; surface smooth or scaly, white to yellowish buff, tending to stain vinaceous over the lower part; margin depressed around the stalk and joined to it when young, sometimes exposing the spore mass by irregular rupture of surrounding tissue; gleba of irregularly folded rudimentary gill plates, pallid to yellow-brown becoming chocolate brown and powdery at maturity; stalk 1–5 cm long, 0.5–2.5 cm thick, white or stained like the cap. Edibility is unknown. (AMD)

Endoptychum depressum

COMMENTS   Found fruiting in late fall under ponderosa pine of the Transition zone as well as aspen and mixed conifers of the Canadian zone. It is also described as *Secotium* and *Gyrophragmium* by some authors, as is a related species *E. agaricoides*. *E. agaricoides* is an inhabitant of wastelands and is particularly common in pinyon-juniper woodlands of the Upper Sonoran zone. (LAS, MNA, SWM) A similar species, *E. arizonicum*, has been reported in the Southwest by Smith but I have not as yet encountered it.

Longula texensis (Berk. and Curt.) Zeller

Fruiting body with stalk and cap; cap oval to round or depressed, 3–9 cm broad, 2–7 cm high, scaly becoming smooth in age; margin first joined to the cap by a veil but rupturing in age; flesh firm, white but staining yellow (sometimes pinkish) in bruised areas; gleba of folded, branched brownish plates which become brownish to blackish at maturity, exposed or partly exposed in age; stalk 3–8 cm long, 2–3.5 cm thick, stout, woody when mature, extending through the gleba as a stalk-columella, white or colored like the cap.

Longula texensis

Montagnea arenarius

Podaxis pistillaris

COMMENTS Allied to *Agaricus*, this species is common in the hot desert wastelands (on sandbars of the Grand Canyon of the Colorado and the Rio Grande) and other areas of poor soil. Edibility is unknown.

Montagnea arenarius (D. C.) Zeller

Fruiting bodies 8–30 cm tall, arising from a buried egglike primordium; stalk white, scaly, almost woody on drying, 0.5–2 cm thick, longitudinally striate, splitting into fibrillose scales, stalk base as a small, rounded bulb set in a saclike volva buried in soil, stalk equal or swollen in the middle, dilated at the apex into a rounded disklike cap; cap 1.5–4 cm broad, white to grayish with scattered tissues of the plates attached to the margin; plates crowded, radiating and sickle-shaped with rounded edges.

COMMENTS Also known as *Montagnites*, this agaricoid Gasteromycete is Coprinuslike in general appearance and stature. It is common in sandy desert soils where it is often partly buried by drifting sand. It may occur in great abundance, scattered among cool desert shrubs, producing hundreds of fruiting bodies. (AMD, SNGM)

Podaxis pistillaris (L. ex Pers) Fries

Fruiting body 6–20 cm tall; cap oval to broadly elliptical borne atop a tall slender stalk, whitish to yellow-brown with a whitish coarsely scaly layer that peels away leaving a smooth inner layer; this layer opens by means of splitting and flaking along the lower margin of attachment to the stalk; stalk narrow, 0.5–1.5 cm thick, striate, coarsely fibrous and twisted, somewhat scaly at the top, often swollen at the base; gleba of rudimentary plates containing yellow-brown, reddish brown, or blackish spores. (AMD, LAS)

COMMENTS This fungus is called the "False Shaggy Mane" because it bears a remarkable resemblance to the agaric, *Coprinus comatus*. It grows in sandy soils and frequently appears in the spring along roadways often pushing up through the surfacing. It has been cited as the most common fungus of the hot deserts of the Southwest. (SNGM) *Montagnea arenarius* is similar in appearance when young but the peridium breaks open on the lateral margins leaving an apical button and stalk tissue as attachment points for the gill plates.

Battarrea phalloides (Dicks.) Persoon

Fruiting body stalked, up to 20 cm tall, supporting a terminal puffballlike spore sac; peridium opening around the circumference of the sac base, falling away in a single piece, leaving a shieldlike basal plate atop the stalk; stalk is coarsely fibrous and twisted. (AMD, LAS)

COMMENTS   This is one of the most spectacular of the stalked puffball species found in the Southwest. It is most common in the Great Basin desert and in other cool desert shrublands. It typically grows in sandy soils and its stalk, bleached white by the sun, remains for several months, appearing as a neatly placed stake in the sandy desert soil. A similar species, *B. digueti*, is found in Baja California and northern Mexico. It is distinguished by the several to many pored openings of a persistent peridium, pores through which the spore mass is released at maturity. Abundant fruitings have been noted in salt cedar thickets along the Colorado River and Rio Grande.

Phallus impudicus Persoon

Fruiting body stalked, arising from an egg-shaped primordium; primordium hypogeous and with basal cordlike rhizomorphs; stalk breaking through the apex of the primordium, white, up to 25 cm tall with an apical fertile surface; cap conical with an apical pore and a netlike surface beneath a slimy spore mass, surface resembling the honeycomb pattern of a morel; spore mass olive to grayish brown with an extremely offensive odor. (AMD, LAS)

COMMENTS   In early development, this stinkhorn resembles a morel. However, the basal "egglike primordium" and the foul odor of the spore mass quickly dispel any doubts as to its identity as well as its edibility. It is found on the ground in moist rich humus of deciduous trees and shrubs of the Riparian zone and is the only stinkhorn of any abundance in the Southwest.

Tulostoma and Allies

There are many species of *Tulostoma*, and all are found growing in desert sand and dry soils. Other related stalked puffballs found occasionally in southwestern deserts include *Phellorina strobilina* and *Chlamydopus* spp. (AMD, SNGM)

Battarrea phalloides

Phallus impudicus

Tulostoma poculatum

Tulostoma poculatum White

Fruiting body 3–5 cm tall, consisting of a puffballlike spore sac atop a slender, woody stalk; peridium firm, smooth, cream to buff-colored, membranous, covered initially by an exterior sheath that erodes away to form a cuplike bank of hyphae and sand at its base, opening by a terminal pore; pore with a slightly raised collar, releasing cinnamon-colored spores.

COMMENTS   A large number of similar *Tulostoma* species are found associated with pinyon pine and juniper in the Upper Sonoran zone. These include *T. brumale*, *T. striatum*, *T. opacum*, and *T. simulans*. This last species is more common in the eastern shortgrass prairies. *T. cretaceum* is a common inhabitant of sand dunes. Edibility of these fungi has not been determined. (AMD, LAS)

Crucibulum laeve

Bird's Nest Fungi

The fruiting body of these small gasteromycetes looks like a miniature bird's nest complete with eggs. The eggs are actually spore capsules (peridioles) and the nest a "splash cup." The force of a single raindrop can splash the spore capsules out of the cup to be deposited on various types of organic debris where the decay mycelium develops from the spores.

Crucibulum laeve Kambly

Fruiting bodies small, 5–10 mm tall, 5–10 mm broad at the mouth, peridium broadly vase-shaped or with little or no basal constriction; buff, ocher, or cinnamon brown; inner peridium smooth, shiny, buff-colored; peridioles disk-shaped, 1–2 mm broad, pale white to buff. (BSM, LAS, MNA) COMMENTS   Following monsoon rains, this petite bird's nest fungus grows in conspicuous clusters on dead wood in the pinyon-juniper woodland. It is widespread throughout the conifer and hardwood forests of the Southwest, fruiting from May to October.

Cyathus striatus (Huds.) Persoon

Fruiting body 10–15 mm high, funnel-shaped with a wide mouth; the outer wall firm, cinnamon brown to dark brown, covered with shaggy, woolly hairs; the inner wall hard, smooth, and vertically fluted or ridged; peridioles (eggs) oval, dark, shiny, 2–3 mm broad, positioned in the base of the cup. (LAS)

COMMENTS   A typical "bird's nest" fungus, *Cyathus* is found on dead hardwood and decaying leaves under deciduous trees. Another common species is *C. stercorius* which grows on manure and organic debris. (AMD)

Scleroderma hypogaeum Zeller

Fruiting body 2–10 cm broad, subglobose, with a short stumplike base in larger specimens, tapering toward the top with prominent folds and furrows in the peridial wall; peridium white becoming ochraceous, staining vinaceous, firm and cartilaginous at first, then smooth and hard in age, opening by cracks to expose the dark yellow-brown to black glebal tissue inside; odor unpleasant and pervading; spore mass black and powdery at maturity.

Cyathus striatus

Scleroderma hypogaeum

COMMENTS   As is typical of other species of *Scleroderma*, their peridial wall is rigid and firm. The fruiting bodies are hypogeous under the leaf litter of conifers, particularly pine. *S. citrinum* (*S. aurantiacum*) has also been found in the Southwest in sandy soil. (BSM, LAS, MNA, MSM) Sclerodermas are often confused with the soft-skinned puffballs of the genus *Lycoperdon*, but they are clearly different in the firm texture of the peridium and the colored glebal spore mass in youth. They are not recommended edibles since some have been reported to cause gastric upset.

Scleroderma michiganense (Guzman) Guzman

Fruiting body typically hypogeous, 3–9 cm broad, subglobose, with or without a short basal extension; surface smooth or minutely scaly; wall up to 2.5 mm thick and hard; white staining pinkish vinaceous, becoming buff on drying; copious white cordlike basal rhizomorphs; gleba yellowish brown, coal black at maturity interspersed with fine white fibers.

COMMENTS   Found in the fall under hardwoods of the Riparian zone. No hard-skinned puffballs should be eaten.

Scleroderma michiganense

Geastrum and Allies

Of the many species of earthstars known, the majority occur in the Southwest. They are modified puffballs in which the outer skin splits into starlike rays. Species of *Geastrum* are difficult to identify without the use of microscopic features. Their look-alike, *Astreus*, has spongy tissue surrounding the outside of the spore sac and differs in a number of microscopic features as well.

Astreus hygrometricus Morgan

Fruiting body round, up to 5 cm broad, composed of two white peridial layers; outer peridial layer splitting at maturity into 6–15 starlike rays; rays becoming recurved below the inner peridium on drying thereby raising it upwards; inner peridium puffball-shaped, whitish to brownish gray, opening by an irregular pore or slit at the apex to release dark brown spores. (LAS, SWM)

COMMENTS   *Astreus* resembles an earthstar but its hard outer peridium places it with the sclerodermas which are "hard-skinned" puffballs. It differs from sclerodermas in the rays, which split open and curl back when wet and close again when dry. Even in dry years this species fruits in poor soils of open meadows, road margins and exposed sites. It is a species well adapted for the drier sites of the Upper Sonoran and Transition zones.

Geastrum fimbriatum Fries

Fruiting body 1–2 cm broad; outer peridium cream to pale tan, splitting into 5–10 (12) rays; rays with acute tips, split halfway to the base, and smooth in the bowl; fleshy inner peridium; grayish tan to dark brown; pore mouth without a distinct boundary line; spore mass dark brown and powdery. (SNGM)

COMMENTS   *G. fimbriatum* is similar to *G. saccatum* (MNA, MSM), which has defined pore mouths, and *G. triplex* (LAS, MNA), which has a cuplike collar that surrounds the inner peridium and only a slightly raised pore mouth. All three species are found in aspen and mixed conifer forests of the Canadian and Hudsonian zone.

Astreus hygrometricus

Geastrum fimbriatum

Geastrum fornicatum

Lycoperdon perlatum

Geastrum fornicatum (Huds.) Fries

Fruiting body 2–2.5 cm broad, round or flattened when unopened, encrusted with debris; outer peridium splitting into 4–7 rays; rays ocherbrown or pinkish tan, upright then peeling back under until they are nearly erect; the exposed dark brown ray tissue peeling off in patches to reveal paler brown tissue underneath; inner peridium (spore case) roundish to compressed, with large torn mouthlike opening at top, mounted on a short stalk (pedicel); surface brown to dark brown. (AMD, LAS)

COMMENTS   This earthstar is frequently found in the pinyon-juniper woodland of the Upper Sonoran zone. Other species that may be encountered in mixed conifer forests include *G. minimum, G. mammosum, G. rufescens,* and *G. xerophilum,* which is also common in the desert. (AMD)

Lycoperdon perlatum Persoon

Fruiting body pear-shaped, 2–6 cm broad, up to 8 cm tall, saclike and rounded at the apex, with a stumplike base or pseudostem; outer peridium pure white when young, developing small but abundant cone-shaped spines that turn brown and fall away at maturity, leaving scars of the peridium; inner peridium smooth, white at first, then brown and papery at maturity; gleba white, then olive-brown with the development of the spore mass; spore mass wet at first, then powdery, released through a ragged hole in the apex of the inner peridium. (BSM, LAS, MNA, MSM)

COMMENTS   As a typical puffball, *L. perlatum* is widespread, occurring on the ground under both conifers and hardwoods. It fruits in early summer and continues through the growing season. Its edibility is good if prepared when the gleba is still pure white. *L. pyriforme,* a pear-shaped puffball, is a smaller species growing at somewhat higher elevations on decayed hardwood logs in clusters. I find its edibility superior to that of *L. perlatum.* (BSM, LAS, MNA, MSM)

Calbovista subsculpta Morse

Fruiting bodies 6–16 cm broad, nearly round when young becoming broader than tall, with a sterile base or pseudostalk; peridium white to light yellow-brown in age, breaking up into irregular patches up to 8 mm thick; gleba white becoming dark brown to purplish brown as the spores mature. (LAS, MSM, SWM)

Calbovista subsculpta

COMMENTS   Called the "Sculptured Puffball," this species is one of the most frequently encountered of the giant puffballs and is found in open meadows of the high-elevation forests. It fruits in summer and early fall following monsoon rains. It is edible as long as the spore mass remains white. *Calvatia subcretacea* is similarly sculptured, but it is smaller, base-ball-sized, and lacks a pseudostalk. The golf-ball–sized *C. fumosa* is patterned at maturity with cracks and small scales. It has an extremely foul odor. Both are inhabitants of the Hudsonian zone. Edibility is questionable. (MNA)

Calvatia booniana A. H. Smith

Fruiting body developing rapidly from a small round primordium to large proportions, up to 60 cm broad and 30 cm high; lacking a sterile pseudo-stalk; peridium sculptured and separating into large, flat polygonal scales, dull white to unevenly brown; gleba olive-brown to brown; odor strong and unpleasant when mature. (LAS, MNA, MSM, SWM)

Calvatia booniana

Calvatia cyathiformis

COMMENTS   *C. booniana* is called the "Western Giant Puffball." It has a good flavor when young, and an average size fruiting body provides plenty to eat. It is common in the sagebrush flats adjoining Riparian habitats that extend into forested areas. It fruits in midsummer to fall.

Calvatia cyathiformis (Bosc.) Morgan

Fruiting body 5–20 cm high, 5–16 cm broad at greatest diameter, tapered to a narrow rootlike attachment, top-shaped or pear-shaped; outer peridium whitish, flaking away to expose a purplish tan to purplish brown inner layer; both layers finally eroding and cracking to expose the gleba; gleba somewhat cottony, yellowish then brownish, and finally dull purple with purple spores.

COMMENTS   Apparently widely scattered in grassy areas of the Sonoran zone and grasslands. The similar *C. craniiformis* has greenish yellow to yellow-brown gleba and is found in the Riparian zone and oak woodlands.

Sac Fungi

CUP FUNGI, SADDLE FUNGI, AND MORELS

The majority of fungi belong to the class Ascomycetes, but most species appear in their microscopic, asexual form as molds, mildews, or yeasts. The large, fleshy fruiting bodies are formed only in a limited number of families. Of these, the family Pezizaceae, which contains the common cup fungi, saddle fungi, and morels is the most frequently encountered and actively sought group. Stalked cup fungi, which are tough and gelatinous, belong to the family Sarcocyphaceae. They are often found on wood and fruit throughout the summer. The morels of the family Morchellaceae are without rival as a seasonally abundant edible. They appear in a variety of forested habitats during the spring and early summer. The flesh of the fruiting bodies is cartilaginous to firm and brittle, crumbling into irregular fragments when pressed or squeezed. Morels have a characteristic flavor, often described as "rich mushroomy and nutlike." Some of the false morels and saddle fungi are poisonous and are best avoided as a group. The brilliant and variously colored species of *Hypomyces* are moldlike, parasites of fleshy mushrooms, taking the shape of their mushroom host as they grow over the fruiting body surface.

Fruiting bodies of some Ascomycetes, like *Sarcosphaera*, develop partly submerged in the soil and litter but later emerge to expose the fertile tissue to disperse the spores. Others remain underground throughout development with the fertile tissue enclosed at maturity. These hypogeous, tuber-like Ascomycetes are commonly known as "truffles" and they are treated in a separate section.

Key to the Ascomycetes

1a. Fruiting body hypogeous; typically tuberous; hymenium enclosed at maturity; the interior a hollow cavity(ies), (filled with powdery spores in *Elaphomyces*), or solid and marbled with veins . . . .
. . . . (p. 186) Tuberlike fungi
1b. Fruiting body epigeous, hymenium exposed at maturity 2
    2a. Fruiting body as small pimplelike *perithecia* embedded in a white, golden yellow, orange, reddish orange, or yellowish green layer of mycelium that covers the surface of mushrooms as a parasite . . . . . (pp. 177, 179) *Hypomyces* spp.
    2b. Not as above 3
3a. Fruiting body cup-shaped; stalk lacking or if present short with ribs
. . . . 7
3b. Not as above 4
    4a. Fruiting bodies as elongated, ear-shaped stalks . . . .
. . . . (p. 183) *Otidea leporina*
    4b. Fruiting bodies with a stalk bearing caps of various shapes
. . . . 5
5a. Caps bell-shaped with a honeycomb pattern of ridges and pits . . . .
. . . . (pp. 179, 181) *Morchella* spp.
5b. Caps brain-shaped or saddle-shaped without definite pits 6
    6a. Caps brain-shaped; tissues as wrinkled or convoluted folds
. . . . (pp. 173, 174) *Gyromitra* spp.
    6b. Caps saddle-shaped; tissue folds broad . . . .
. . . . (p. 176) *Helvella lacunosa*
7a. Cup brown above, paler at base, conspicuously ribbed, stalk present or absent . . . . (p. 174) *Helvella acetabulum*
7b. Cup fleshy to brittle; variously colored, stalk inconspicuous or absent 8
    8a. Cup large, partly hypogeous and splitting open into a series of pointed rays . . . . (p. 183) *Sarcosphaera crassa*
    8b. Not as above 9
9a. Cup tan to brown; margin typically expanding outward to form a disk . . . . (p. 183) *Peziza repanda*
9b. Cup red-colored with hairy margins . . (p. 185) *Scutellinia scutellata*

Gyromitra gigas

Gyromitra gigas (Krombh.) Quellet

Fruiting bodies 5–7 cm tall, 5–15 cm wide, cap composed of convoluted or folded brainlike tissues supported by a short stalk; fertile, exposed tissue yellowish brown to dark orange-brown, fragile, and crumbly when crushed; stalk short with irregular folds, the cap tissue closely pressed around it. (LAS, MNA, MSM)

COMMENTS   The fruiting bodies of this "False Morel" are found in the spring around the margins of melting snowbanks of the Canadian and Hudsonian zones. It is associated with decayed wood and humus of conifers and is called the "Snow Mushroom" by some authors. (SNGM) It is reportedly edible as is its look-alike, *G. esculenta*, which has a wrinkled, lobed cap, and occurs in mixed pine and aspen. (AMD, MSM) If these mushrooms are to be eaten, they should be cooked to release the toxin, monomethylhydrazine. Because we know very little about the consequences of consuming these fungi, they cannot be recommended for the table.

Gyromitra infula

Gyromitra infula (Shaeff. ex Fr.) Quell

Fruiting body 6–15 cm tall, stalked with an irregularly lobed often saddle-shaped cap; cap deep reddish brown, surfaces smooth and convoluted with free undulating margins; stalk white to light brown, unribbed, hollow. (BSM, LAS, MNA, MSM)

COMMENTS   The saddle-shaped to irregularly lobed fruiting bodies of this poisonous false morel are found on rotting wood and humus in both hardwood and conifer forests. *G. infula* is widely distributed. Unlike other Gyromitras of the region, this one fruits in summer and fall.

Helvella acetabulum (L. ex Fr.) Quellet

Cup 2–8 cm broad, 1–4 cm high, bowl-shaped, edges rolled inward when young and later expanding; exterior brown above and white to cream-colored at base, conspicuously ribbed, surface smooth or finely hairy; interior light brown and chambered at the base; stalk usually present, short and chambered in cross section.

COMMENTS   Fruits separately on ground or from well-decayed wood in both deciduous and coniferous forests. Edibility unknown.

Helvella acetabulum

Helvella lacunosa

Helvella lacunosa Afz. ex Fr.

Fruiting body 8–15 cm tall; cap grayish black, with convoluted lobes, somewhat saddle-shaped, attached to the stalk in places; stalk white, prominently ribbed, the ribs often forming deep elongated pockets, expanded toward the base, up to 12 cm long, chambered inside. (BSM, LAS, MNA, MSM, SWM)

COMMENTS   The black Helvellas are difficult to identify but *H. lacunosa* is the most common species in the Southwest. It is easily distinguished from two other frequently encountered species, *H. crispa*, which has a white, fluted stalk and white to cream-colored cap (BSM, LAS), and *H. compressa*, which has a nonribbed stalk and yellowish brown cap. (AMD) *H. lacunosa* fruits in early spring in both hardwood and conifer forests. All three have been collected in late summer and early fall, especially in the spruce-fir forests of the Canadian and Hudsonian zones.

Hypomyces lactifluorum

Hypomyces spp.

The presence of this parasitic sac fungus cannot go unnoticed by anyone who collects species of *Russula* and *Lactarius*. Several species of *Hypomyces* are involved; each produces a characteristic and colorful mycelium that covers the surface of the mushroom host. The mycelium causes the host to be unrecognizable by covering the gills and leaving only ridges and folds. They are edible if found on an edible mushroom. But since it is possible that a poisonous species could be parasitized, they are not recommended for consumption.

Hypomyces lactifluorum (Schw.) Tul.

A bright orange-red parasite which most frequently attacks *Russula brevipes* in the Southwest (see p. 78). The minute bumps over the surface of the leathery mycelium represent the reproductive vessels, which contain asci with ascospores. It is often called the "Lobster Mushroom." (BSM, LAS, MNA, MSM)

Hypomyces luteovirens

Morchella deliciosa group

Hypomyces luteovirens (Fr.) Tul.

A yellowish green parasite, which is often found on *Russula* species. The small, bumpy reproductive vessels are more conspicuous than those of *H. lactifluorum*. In the Southwest, it is found most frequently on red-colored species of *Russula*.

Morchella deliciosa group

Fruiting body 3–8 cm tall; caps conical to rounded at the apex, heavily pitted with the outer margins of the pits cream-colored and the interior brown to dark brown; stalk white to cream-colored, hollow. (MNA)
COMMENTS   The "White Morel," like the yellow morel, is associated with hardwood trees and shrubs of the Riparian zone. The southwestern variety is more robust with cream-colored margins than the typical species. Some authors consider it a dark, immature form of *M. esculenta*.

Morchella elata group

Fruiting body 3–10 cm tall; cap gray brown to dark brown, narrowly to broadly conical with deep honeycomb-patterned pits; the pit ridges often longitudinally arranged and become blackish in age; cap supported by a white to cream-colored stalk unevenly ribbed, coated with small white granules or warts, hollow into the cap region. (BSM, LAS, MNA, MSM)
COMMENTS   The "Black Morels" are a highly variable group of mushrooms that may represent a number of separate species. Characteristics of *M. elata* overlap those of *M. angusticeps* (MNA, SWM) and of *M. conica*, the European black morel. (AMD, LAS) *M. conica* is considered by some authors to be a dark variety of *M. esculenta*, the yellow morel. *M. angusticeps* fruits in the spring, but it may also appear sporadically in the summer. It is associated with aspen and pine at the edges of meadows, open areas, and in forested areas recently burned. The black morel should be regarded with caution when eaten in large quantities or consumed with alcoholic beverages. Poisoning can result, but the response varies greatly with individuals. All morels are regarded as exceptionally good edibles. The edibles are easily recognized once the features of the poisonous look-alikes are known. Species of *Verpa* have short, hollow, conical caps that are free from the stalk except at the apex and often with wrinkled or ridged surfaces without

Morchella elata

Morchella esculenta

pits. *Verpa bohemica* occurs in the chaparral of the Upper Sonoran zone. (AMD, LAS, MNA, MSM) Other look-alikes include Gyromitras with large brainlike caps (described earlier) and to some degree the stinkhorn, *Phallus impudicus*.

Morchella esculenta L. ex Fr.

Fruiting body 7–20 cm tall, yellowish cream to light brownish yellow; cap broadly conical at the apex, oval to elongate in form with deep irregular pits; stalk white with granular ribs or unevenly smooth, hollow into the interior of the cap region. (LAS, MNA, MSM)

COMMENTS   The "Yellow Morel" fruits in the spring, which in the South-west is usually a dry season. Therefore it appears sporadically, when moisture is available, in association with hardwood trees of the Riparian zone, especially alder, sycamore, and poplar. The fruiting period lasts about two weeks, and I have found some specimens to attain spectacular proportions, up to 40 cm tall and 22 cm wide.

Otidea leporina

Peziza repanda

Otidea leporina (Fr.) Fuckel

Fruiting bodies 1–4 cm tall, 1–2 cm broad, erect, vertically folded with a split on one side resembling a rabbit's ear; outer surface light brown to brown, inner surface cream to pale yellowish brown. (LAS)

COMMENTS   Of the several ascomycetes that are ear-shaped, this species is the most common in the Southwest. It fruits in late summer and fall under oak and pine in the Transition zone. Its edibility is unknown. *Otidea alutacea* is a clustered, brown-colored species associated with Douglas fir in the Canadian zone. (AMD)

Peziza repanda Fries

Fruiting body cuplike, stalk absent; cup smooth with even margin when young, 2–10 cm broad, becoming recurved to nearly flat with a wavy torn margin; interior pale tan; exterior pale tan and covered with white powdery granules. (LAS, MSM)

COMMENTS   This common cup-fungus occurs on decaying wood and on beds of rich humus and occasionally on the ground. Edibility of Pezizas is unknown. Other cup-fungus look-alikes that also occur in the Southwest include: *Discina perlata* with a wrinkled inner surface and a short stalk, found under conifers of the Hudsonian zone (LAS, MNA, MSM); *Helvella (Paxina) acetabulum* with prominent whitish veins or ribs extending upwards from the cup stalk found in mixed aspen-conifer forests. (LAS, MNA)

Sarcosphaera crassa (Sant. ex Steud.) Pouz.

Fruiting body as a large cup, 3–10 cm broad, partly buried in the soil when young; the margin even at first, then splitting outward into 6–10 starlike fleshy rays, inner cup surface pink to pinkish violet, outer cup surface faded pink to grayish lilac. (LAS, MNA, MSM, SWM)

COMMENTS   Known as the "Pink Crown," this species is reported to be a good edible, but caution is advised if eaten without cooking first. Also known as *S. exima* and *S. coronaria*, it is found singly or in groups under hardwoods and conifers in the wetter sites of the Canadian and Transition zones following periods of heavy precipitation.

Sarcosphaera crassa

Scutellinia scutellata

Scutellinia scutellata (L. ex Fr.) Lamb

Fruiting bodies as small cups, 5–20 mm; cup shallow becoming flat; margin fringed with dark brown to black hairs, inner surface bright reddish orange to red.

COMMENTS   Although there are several brightly colored cup-fungi associated with decayed conifer wood, this species is distinctive because of its eyelashlike hairs that border the cup. It demonstrates a preference for old logs that have been burned. Other colorful cup fungi that can be found in the Southwest include: *Aleuria aurantia* with bright orange cups with wavy margins and stalkless. (LAS, MNA, MSM) *Sarcoscypha coccinea* with stalked cup that is externally whitish with a brilliant scarlet inner surface (AMD, BSM, MNA); and *Bisporella citrina* (*Helotium citrinum*) with a bright yellow cup clustered in masses on decayed wood. (BSM, LAS, MNA)

Truffles and False Truffles

Truffles are the subterranean or hypogeous fruiting bodies of a variety of fungus groups. The fruiting bodies develop beneath litter and in the mineral soil of the forest floor, and their spore mass is protected and enclosed by a peridium. Truffles vary in size from that of a pea to as large as a grapefruit. Most are the size of a small potato tuber and even possess the dimples and depressions that are typical of a potato. Truffles are some of the most fascinating fungi to be found, not only because of their reputation as a culinary delicacy, but because the majority of them form economically and biologically important relationships with the roots of trees as mycorrhizae. Many of the epigeous fungi that form mycorrhizae also have a truffle relative.

Mycologists have suggested that the truffle growth-form is an adaptation for successful reproduction under moisture-limiting conditions that would otherwise prevent epigeous development. Spore dispersal from the mature fruiting body is accomplished through mycophagy since a subterranean position precludes spore discharge into the air. Attracted by odors released from the truffle at maturity, small mammals and insects quickly find and consume the fruiting body. The spores are deposited in the feces, presumably unharmed in their journey through the digestive tract, and upon germination are capable of establishing a mycorrhizal relationship with a nearby root system.

Ascomycetes of the order Tuberales are considered to be true truffles. The sacs (asci) containing ascospores are borne on convoluted tissues within the gleba. These tissues are fleshy and brittle and often have a characteristic combination of mushroom and nutlike flavors. Several species of the genus *Tuber*, the much publicized truffle of southern Europe, have been found to occur in the Southwest. They are generally smaller than the European species and their flavor is less pronounced.

The majority of hypogeous fungi are Basidiomycetes and are called false truffles. The gleba is chambered (pored), rather than hollow, or filled with convoluted tissues as in most truffles. The tissues are usually firm and cartilaginous as opposed to the fleshy, brittle texture of the truffles. In many species the gleba disintegrates into a gelatinous, slimy, odorous spore mass. The flavor, much like that of the odor, is either penetrating and unpleasant, or bland and nondescript. Small mammals find them more delectable than mushrooms and consume all species without apparent preference.

Despite their hidden position, truffles are not difficult to find. Most are formed in the humus layer of the forest litter, or between the litter layer and the mineral soil. Some are buried in the loose mineral soil but unlike the European Tubers, they are quite close to or exposed at the surface. A small garden cultivator with four to five tines can be used to rake away the soil and litter to reveal the fruiting bodies scattered among the fine feeder roots of the tree host. The excavations of animals can be used as indicators for truffle sites. The variety and abundance of truffles in the coniferous forests of the Southwest are equal to those found in almost any other region of the United States.

Key to the Tuberlike Fungi

1a. Fruiting bodies fleshy to firm when young (becoming bone hard in *Elaphomyces*); interior of either convoluted folds and marbled veins of tissue or hollow with one to several chambers stuffed with cottony hyphae; sterile base or columella absent; peridium in some ornamented with small warts; spores borne inside asci (Truffles) 2

1b. Fruiting bodies firm, cartilaginous when young; interior with or without a sterile base or columella, with uniform spore-bearing tissue or with spongelike poroid chambers, gelatinizing at maturity in some species; peridium often covered with threadlike rhizomorphs; spores borne on basidia (False Truffles) 4

    2a. Fruiting body dark brown, hairy (tomentose); peridium eroding to expose an extensively convoluted interior; interior white with colored veins . . . .
    . . . . (p. 193) *Geopora cooperi* and relatives

2b. Not as above 3
3a. Fruiting body round, firm, becoming bone hard; interior dark-colored at maturity . . . . (p. 190) *Elaphomyces*
3b. Fruiting body round to lobed, fleshy, but firm; interior fertile tissue remaining light-colored or as dark veins at maturity . . . .
. . . . (p. 203) *Tuber levissimum* and relatives
    4a. Columella present (as exposed by longitudinal sectioning through the center of the fruiting body) 5
    4b. Columella typically absent or rudimentary 11
5a. Peridial wall up to 5 mm thick; gleba as gill-like plates attached to a prominent basal, stumplike columella . . . .
. . . . (see p. 151) *Radiigera atrogleba*
5b. Not as above 6
    6a. Columella stalklike or as a prominent basal cushion . . . 7
    6b. Columella not stalklike but often conspicuous and branched 8
7a. Peridium bright yellow to grayish olive; gleba composed of tubular chambers separated by branches of the stalk-columella . . . .
. . . . (p. 201) *Truncocolumella citrina*
7b. Peridium white, staining bright blue on bruising; basal columella unbranched; gleba minutely chambered . . . .
. . . . (p. 189) *Chamonixia brevicolumna*
    8a. Peridium reduced or absent; exposed gleba light pinkish brown to brown, cartilaginous, conspicuously chambered with a white, branched columella . . . .
    . . . . (pp. 190, 193) *Gautieria* spp.
    8b. Not as above 9
9a. Peridium white bruising pinkish, splitting and separable from a cartilaginous, rubbery gleba; columella prominent and branched . . . .
. . . . (p. 194) *Hysterangium separabile*
9b. Not as above 10
    10a. Peridium white becoming orange-brown at maturity, tough and skinlike; gleba yellow to ocher; gleba a crumbly spore mass at maturity   (p. 201) *Sclerogaster xerophilum*
    10b. Peridium white becoming some shade of brown but not orange, soft and fleshy, easily bruised; gleba chambered and spongy . . . . (p. 194) *Hymenogaster sublilacinus*
11a. Glebal chambers persistent, filled with gel at maturity 12

11b. Glebal chambers not gel-filled at maturity but sometimes becoming
      entirely gelatinous including chamber walls . . . .
      . . . . (pp. 197, 199, 200) *Rhizopogon* spp.

  12a. Gleba white to light cream with whitish veins; peridium
        white to yellowish . (p. 196) *Leucogaster* and *Leucophleps*

  12b. Gleba brown to black with whitish to yellow veins; per-
        idium brownish yellow, brown to dark reddish brown . . .
        . . . . (p. 196) *Melanogaster tuberiformis*

Chamonixia brevicolumna

Chamonixia brevicolumna Smith and Singer

Fruiting body 1–3 cm broad, generally round in shape but irregular in
contour with depressions and furrows especially near the base; base as a
short stumplike columella extending into the gleba as a white sterile plug;
peridium white, becoming olive-yellow, sparsely covered with fine rhizomorphs; bruising and staining dark blue; gleba firm and finely poroid,
reddish cinnamon, staining blue when cut. (SNGM)

COMMENTS   The identity of this false truffle is easily confirmed by the rapid and intense blue reaction to bruising and the sterile basal plug outlined against reddish cinnamon gleba. It is associated with spruce and subalpine fir in the Hudsonian zone.

Elaphomyces granulatus Fries

Fruiting body smooth; hard, round, 0.5–2.5 cm diameter; peridium pallid, tawny yellow or dull gold drying rusty brown, ornamented with minute slightly raised pyramidal warts appearing in some specimens as superficial dark spots, thick-walled, composed of several differently shaded layers enclosing the gleba; gleba gray-brown to black becoming powdery and separating as a mass from the peridium at maturity. (AMD)

COMMENTS   A complex of species, all similar in appearance, has been described in *Elaphomyces*. They are abundantly produced in association with the roots of lodgepole and ponderosa pine of the Transition zone. Some species commonly occur under firs in the Hudsonian zone. Lincoff (LAS) reports its use as an aphrodisiac in England. It is easy to identify with its marblelike hardness and shape.

Gautieria gautieroides (Lloyd) Zeller & Dodge

Fruiting bodies 2–5 cm broad, rounded, with a short stumplike base with conspicuous rhizomorphs; peridium a white, filmy weft of hyphae that disappears at maturity to expose the chambered gleba; chamber walls lined with spores, gleba ochraceous to cinnamon-brown, tough to cartilaginous with a white translucent branched columella, crisp on cutting, odor nauseatingly sweet and musty.

COMMENTS   Several other species of *Gautieria* are common in the mixed conifer forests of the Southwest, among them *G. monticola* (SNGM) and *G. crispa* (provisional name), described below. They fruit in both spring and fall, sometimes in such quantity that one can literally fill bushel baskets. They often emerge from the leaf litter layer but are also buried in the mineral soil. Their flavor is uninteresting and their edibility has not been established. Because of their cartilaginous consistency, even the small mammals consume them only when no other fungus choice is available.

Elaphomyces granulatus

Gautieria gautieroides

Gautieria crispa

Geopora cooperi

Gautieria crispa Stewart & Trappe prov. nom

Fruiting bodies variable in size, 0.5–6 cm broad, subspherical to irregularly lobed, often apically flattened, thinly covered with a white, silky weft of hyphae but soon disappearing, leaving the chambered gleba exposed; conspicuous basal cordlike rhizomorph; gleba tough, cartilaginous, crisp on cutting, dull white, thin pinkish buff to pinkish ocher as the spore matures, finally light cinnamon at maturity, bruising greenish yellow to amber yellow; glebal chambers elongate-angular, wet when sectioned; central columella whitish or translucent, with profuse branches that become progressively thinner toward the outer margin; odor sweet musky, reminiscent of barley malt.

COMMENTS   Massive fruitings of this species have been collected in the Transition zone where it is associated with lodgepole and ponderosa pine. It tends to be gregarious, forming large subterranean cauliflowerlike clusters. Edibility is unknown.

Geopora cooperi Harkness

Fruiting body pale to dark brown, 2–6 cm broad, surface uneven and lobed, generally round overall, covered with fine, dark brown hairs; the inner fertile area pure white to cream-colored or brownish, with deeply convoluted folds that extend to the surface causing it to appear unevenly furrowed; odor strong and nutlike at maturity. (LAS)

COMMENTS   *Geopora* can be found growing close to the soil surface or beneath leaf litter in mixed conifer-hardwood stands. It is edible but it is difficult to separate the soil debris from the fuzzy, furrowed surface. *Hydnotrya* species are similar in appearance but are smaller, the glebal folds are less pronounced but often more colored (pinkish orange to pinkish cinnamon), and no dark hairs are present on the peridium. The two most frequently encountered species, the salmon to pinkish tan *H. variiformis* and the dark brown to dark reddish brown *H. cerebriformis*, are found in early summer in mixed stands of conifers in the Hudsonian and Canadian zones usually beneath rotten logs and in highly organic soil. Edibility of these species is unknown.

The "geode truffles," *Genaea* spp. and *Genabea* spp. (AMD, SNGM), produce variously lobed, light ocher to blackish brown fruiting bodies. The peridium is warted and the gleba is either hollow and warted or folded with canals extending to the outside. They are found associated with oak and other deciduous trees in the Riparian zone.

Hymenogaster sublilacinus Smith

Fruiting body 2–4 cm broad, sometimes larger, rounded and irregularly lobed when several are fused together; rhizomorphs basally attached and inconspicuous; peridium light brownish yellow to dark brown, quickly bruising brown; gleba firm when cut and exuding clear fluid, rich rusty brown with empty chambers; columella basal, radiating as whitish streaks upwards into the glebal tissue; odor aromatic and penetrating. (SNGM)
COMMENTS   *Hymenogaster* species are associated with coniferous trees and fruit in both spring and fall seasons. The smaller *H. parksii* is more variable in shape and has dark brown gleba. (SNGM)

Hysterangium spp.

Individual species can be identified only by microscopic examination. They are not recommended as edible, although they are not known to be poisonous.

Hysterangium separabile Zeller

Fruiting bodies small, 0.5–2.5 cm broad, round to oval with basal rhizomorphs; peridium white at maturity and bruising pink or dingy brown, often brittle and separable from the gleba and splitting in sections on drying; gleba firm and rubbery, fertile portion pale bluish green to greenish gray, darkening to greenish black, soft and gelatinous in age, marbled by translucent veins radiating from the basal mature spore mass, olive to gray-brown, odor strong and disagreeable when mature; taste somewhat bitter. (SNGM)
COMMENTS   Now classified by some as *H. coriaceum*, the fruiting bodies are scattered or in clusters associated with a dense white mass of mycelium that occupies broad areas in soil and litter beneath coniferous trees and occasionally oak. As one of the most common false truffles of the Southwest, they can be found throughout the year, sometimes in large quantities. Squirrels have been observed to retrieve the fruiting bodies from beneath the winter snow pack.

Hymenogaster sublilacinus

Hysterangium separabile

Leucogaster rubescens

Leucogaster rubescens Zeller and Dodge

Fruiting body 1–3 cm broad, irregularly lobed, white becoming ochraceous to brownish, bruising pink to reddish; peridium smooth, moist when fresh; gleba chalk white to cream-colored, marbled with gel-filled cavities. (SNGM)

COMMENTS   In early spring and summer, this species fruits, sometimes in abundance, under mixed conifers of the Canadian and Hudsonian zones. A look-alike, *Leucophleps spinospora*, does not bruise pink, and the glebal chambers exude a white latex when cut. It also occurs in high-elevation, mixed conifer forests. It has a strong spermatic odor. (SNGM)

Melanogaster tuberiformis Corda

Fruiting bodies rounded, variously shaped according to position in soil or beneath litter, 1–8.5 cm broad; peridium smooth, olive-brown to rusty brown, sparsely covered with dark brown rhizomorphs; gleba dark olive to black with yellowish veins; chambers filled with spores in a slimy gel; odor musty and disagreeable; edibility unknown.

COMMENTS   In the Southwest, most species of *Melanogaster* are most commonly associated with conifers, especially pine. They can be distinguished from one another only by microscopic features. (SNGM)

Rhizopogon evadens A. H. Smith

Fruiting bodies 2–5 cm broad, rounded, irregularly lobed and wrinkled with dimpled depressions when compressed by the soil; peridium white with light yellow to brown stains, bruising pink to red; lightly covered with rhizomorphs, firmly attached to the gleba; gleba without a columella, white changing to olive or olive-brown when mature, gelatinizing with age, odor and taste unpleasant. (SNGM)

COMMENTS   In some years this species is the most abundant and widely distributed false truffle in the coniferous forests of the Southwest. It typically occurs in association with the roots of ponderosa pine and lodgepole pine in the Transition zone. A lookalike, *R. rubescens* is also associated with lodgepole pine. (SNGM)

Melanogaster tuberiformis

Rhizopogon evadens

Rhizopogon ochraceorubens

Rhizopogon ochraceorubens Smith

Fruiting bodies 2–6 cm broad, the round to oblong surface covered by a dense network of yellow to golden brown rhizomorphs; peridium yellow-brown with reddish pigment developing in age; gleba firm and crisp when sectioned, olive to brownish olive. (SNGM)

COMMENTS   This species, like *R. evadens*, occurs in association with pines in the Transition zone. It fruits in late summer and is one of the most common false truffles in the Sierra Madre Occidental of Mexico. *R. occidentalis*, a look-alike, is bright yellow when young and coated with reddish brown strands. It is common in conifer woods on the northern Rockies and Pacific Northwest. (LAS, MSM)

Rhizopogon pinyonensis Harrison and Smith

Fruiting bodies 2–5 cm broad with conspicuous basal rhizomorphs; peridium white to cream-colored, overlaid with fawn-colored rhizomorphs, thick and remaining intact after the gleba gelatinizes; gleba light brown to brown.

Rhizopogon pinyonensis

COMMENTS   This species is typically found in pinyon-juniper woodlands of the Upper Sonoran zone. It is most likely a mycorrhizal associate of pinyon pine. Look-alikes include the smaller *R. subcaerulescens*, which is covered by a dense layer of rhizomorphs and is associated with ponderosa and lodgepole pine, and *R. fallax*, which is associated with the white pines of the Canadian and Hudsonian zones. (SNGM)

Rhizopogon subcaerulescens Smith

Fruiting bodies generally small, round to oval but variously shaped as compressed by soil, 0.2–2.5 cm broad, white, grayish white to buff, becoming buff brown in age; surface densely overlain with white to olive-ocher rhizomorphs; rhizomorphs especially matted and branched at the base of the fruiting body, turning olive green to slate black in potassium hydroxide solution; gleba pale vinaceous buff to wood brown, firm when young, gelatinizing in age and separating from the wall, which remains intact.

COMMENTS   This small white *Rhizopogon* often fruits in the litter layer beneath a variety of conifers, especially pine, and is only occasionally found buried in soil. The dense network of rhizomorphs on the peridium distinguishes it from *R. pinyonensis*. (SNGM)

Rhizopogon subcaerulescens

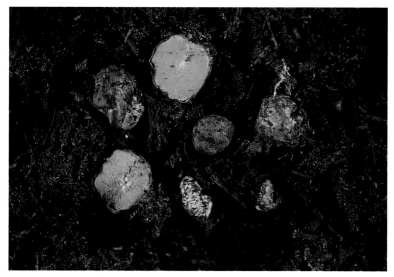

Sclerogaster xerophilum

Sclerogaster xerophilum Fogel

Fruiting bodies rounded, 0.5–2.5 cm broad, occasionally fused together, enmeshed in a thick hyphal mat; white becoming pale yellow or brown; peridium thin and very strong, tearing rather than splitting when sectioned; gleba white in youth becoming bright yellow to brownish orange in age; the spore mass separable from the peridium, dry and crumbly; odor faint to strong and unpleasant.

COMMENTS   This is one of the few false truffles whose fruiting bodies can be found throughout the year. It is primarily associated with the ponderosa and pinyon pines of the Transition and Upper Sonoran zones.

Truncocolumella citrina Zeller

Fruiting body, irregularly lobed, often with a short, thick stalklike base to which are attached conspicuous white rhizomorphs; peridium light to bright lemon yellow becoming dark olive-yellow in age; gleba bluish to brownish olive with conspicuous yellow veins branching from a sterile basal stalk-columella. (LAS)

Truncocolumella citrina

Tuber levissimum

COMMENTS   This brightly colored false truffle is associated with the root system of Douglas fir in the Canadian zone. Its stalk-columella readily distinguishes it from the closely related species of *Rhizopogon*. Its edibility is unknown.

Tuber levissimum Gilkey

Fruiting body 0.5–3.0 cm broad, nearly round with smooth lobed contours, colored light translucent yellow brown to brown on the lobes, white to cream-colored in the surface depressions and furrows; gleba in cross section marbled with tan to gray-brown fertile areas contrasting with white veins; fleshy and brittle; odor and taste mild, richly mushroomlike. I have eaten it and found it good.

COMMENTS   Truffles of this genus are well known both for their edibility and their rarity. Actually, *T. levissimum* can be found in abundance in wet years in late fall and early winter given suitable moisture and temperature conditions. It is associated with ponderosa pine and Douglas fir as a possible mycorrhiza. *T. gibbosum* is a larger look-alike that occurs in the conifer forests of the Pacific coastal region (AMD, MSM), but has not been collected in the Southwest as yet. *T. dryophilum* and *T. rufum* (AMD) occur in mixed pine and oak stands. A similar truffle with a minutely warted reddish peridium and compact marbled gleba is *Balsamia magnata*. (AMD) It is found in both mixed oak and pine forests and in the Riparian zone.

Slime Molds

Slime molds, although small and inconspicuous, are extremely abundant and widespread. They appear on dead and decaying wood or leaves following periods of precipitation and moderate temperatures. Their reproductive structures are colorful, attractively shaped spore cases, *sporangia* if they are stalked, and *aethalia* if without stalks, that bear a powdery mass of spores. They do not provide an edible body, but the feeding stage, a plasmodium, can grow to spectacular proportions in some species. The plasmodium constitutes an unwalled body of protoplasm that slowly moves about, propelled by means of cytoplasmic streaming. Although its motion is not visible, its body forms a noticeable network of veins terminating in a fan-shaped sheet of slime bounded by an invisible membrane. Following a feeding period, during which it consumes microscopic bacteria and organic matter, the plasmodium assembles into a raised, creamy, foamy mound. This mound is then transformed into sporangia and aethalia that are variously shaped and colored depending on the species. Imaginative descriptions of the slime molds have identified them as "creatures from outer space" and the "Dr. Jekylls and Mr. Hydes of the fungus world." Acquiring a collection of these most unique and intriguing fungi can be an enjoyable and intellectually stimulating pastime.

Fuligo septica (L.) Wigg.

Fruiting body an aethalium, 1–15 cm broad, irregularly cushion shaped, produced from a yellow or white shiny or creamy plasmodium; peridium pale brown with yellow tinges below to brown with dull reddish marginal stains; spore mass dark brown to black mixed with white or yellowish lime knots.

Fuligo septica

COMMENTS   *F. septica* is widespread except in the Sonoran zone where *F. megaspora* is common. The plasmodia are highly migratory, moving across the surfaces of downed wood and even standing trees, thereby placing their spore masses in a position for efficient spore dispersal. Many species of slime molds with stalked spore cases are found in southwestern forests, including *Trichia, Hemitrichia, Arcyria,* and *Stemonitis.* (LAS) A sizable field guide could be prepared dealing exclusively with slime molds.

Lycogala epidendrum (L.) Fries

Fruiting bodies puffball-like but small, spherical to somewhat flattened on the bottom; peridium finely warted and pinkish gray to brown, enclosing a bright pink pastelike spore mass; spore mass becoming ochraceous to light pinkish tan, powdery in age. (LAS, MNA)

COMMENTS   This slime mold occurs in clusters on well-rotted logs in mixed deciduous-conifer forests of the Transition, Canadian, and lower Hudsonian zones. It is widespread and one of the easiest slime molds to identify. (LAS)

Lycogala epidendrum

Lichens

Lichens, a symbiotic association of fungus and alga, have a thalloid growth form that can be categorized into three recognizable types: crustose, foliose, and fruiticose. Two major environmental factors that strongly influence the rather cosmopolitan distribution of most lichens are the surfaces to which they are attached and the temperature-moisture gradients, which affect their growth on a local and a seasonal basis. In mountainous areas there is a general increase in numbers of species with increased elevation and associated precipitation. The *crustose* forms are more common in moisture-limited sites and the *foliose* and *fruiticose* types are more common in the moist, shady forests.

Crustose lichens have small thalli with their thallus margins so strongly attached to a rocky or woody substratum that it is difficult to remove them without damage. Because so many species can occupy the same surface, a striking mosaic pattern of lichen colonies is produced. Foliose lichens also lie closely flattened to the substratum, attached by their centers, but with the thallus margins partly free and raised as leafy lobes. Fruiticose lichens have large leafy or bushy thalli often attached at a single point. They are the most conspicuous of the lichens, and because many have the appearance and color of mosses, they are invariably designated as such by the casual observer. Most of the lichen tissue is fungal, and the reproductive structures are often the most striking feature of the thallus. The *apothecia* of ascomycete fungal partners in a lichen are readily comparable in size and color to those found in many of the nonsymbiotic sac fungi. The diverse coloration of lichens is retained on drying. The pigments of some lichens are used by southwestern artisans to dye fabrics. Because of their great abundance in the Southwest, we take lichens for granted. In Europe, lichens are rapidly disappearing because they are intolerant of the effects of acid rain from industry. Where lichens have disappeared, forest trees are dying and with those trees the mycorrhizal mushrooms. Lichens are now endangered species in many areas in Europe. The days of unrestricted collection are over.

Acarospora chlorophana (Ach.) Mass.

Thallus lemon yellow; forming diffuse colonies on acidic rocks, individual colonies 1–2 cm broad, thallus lobes entirely attached; apothecia embedded in the thallus and visible as minute dots on the exposed surface. (HKL) The illustration shows its bright yellow colonies mixed with the leafy greenish gray thalli of *Rhizoplaca chrysoleuca* and the orange-colored colonies of *Candelaria submexicana*.

COMMENTS   Few lichens form such widespread colonies on rock surfaces as does this yellow crustose species. Whole hillsides and cliff faces in the hot southwestern deserts are "painted" with this showy lichen, also known as *A. schleicheri*.

Peltigera maleacea (Ach) Funck

Thallus surface deep green when wet, drying greenish brown, lower surface whitish buff with light central veins and sparse rhizines, partially erect, the lobes upturned and wavy, separating and falling apart when collected. (HKL)

COMMENTS   This common foliose lichen occurs in open grassy areas in conifer stands of the Hudsonian and Canadian zones. As in other species of *Peltigera*, the colonies have a remarkable resemblance to liverworts and are mistakenly considered so by the careless observer. *P. polydactyla* is also common on soil and over mosses in open forests. It has prominent, erect, brown apothecia on the ends of fingerlike lobes.

Physcia caesia (Hoffm.) Hampe

Thallus 4–8 cm broad, whitish mineral gray above, white to buff below; lower surface attached to rock by minute cordlike rhizines; apothecia rare. (HKL)

COMMENTS   The conspicuous thalli of this species are widespread on exposed surfaces of boulders and cliffs of the southwestern deserts.

Acarospora chlorophana

Peltigera maleacea

Physcia caesia

Pseudevernia intensa

Pseudevernia intensa (Nyl.) Hale & Culb.

Thallus dark mineral gray (loosely attached to conifer bark), 5–10 cm broad, lobes flattened, narrow, branched, upper surface smooth to wrinkled, dark brown apothecia common along branch axis; lower surface black at the center and buff to white at the margin. (HKL)

COMMENTS This conspicuous foliose lichen often completely covers the lower, dead branches of spruce and fir in the Canadian and Hudsonian zones. Various species of *Usnea* and *Parmelia* can be found in combination with it. It is restricted in distribution to the Southwest and Mexico.

Usnea arizonica Mot.

Thallus fruiticose, pale greenish yellow, with long cordlike branches; branches with fine hairlike fibrils and papillae (bumps); apothecia disc-shaped, large, up to 10 mm wide, colored as the thallus. (HKL)

COMMENTS *Usnea* is a common fruiticose lichen attached or draped on tree stems and branches. *U. arizonica* is endemic to the Southwest and

Usnea arizonica

Xanthoparmelia lineola

southern California. As an attached form it is easily recognized because of the large, whitish green apothecia fringed with thin, tapered branches. *U. cavernosa* has a large thallus (10–40 cm long) and is also a draped species on conifer branches. *U. hirta* has short thalli, 3–6 cm long, and lacks apothecia.

Xanthoparmelia lineola (Berry) Hale

Thallus growing in more or less circular colonies, yellowish green, 2–15 cm broad, marginal lobes elongate and free, central lobes attached and smaller; the lower surface with hyphal threads (*rhizines*); apothecia central and large, up to 8 mm broad, dark brown. (HKL)

COMMENTS   This foliose lichen grows abundantly on volcanic rocks in the Transition and Upper Sonoran zones. The related *X. chlorochroa* is a nonapothecial lichen that grows in loose, leafy clusters on soil in the Great Basin desert. The upper surface of the thallus is greenish yellow with margins turned under partly covering the dark brown lower surface. It is used as a dye source by native Americans.

Xanthoria elegans

Xanthoria elegans (Link) Th. Fries

Thallus 2.5 cm broad, bright orange, closely attached to rock surfaces, lower surface white, with short hyphal strands (rhizines); apothecia abundant and crowded, colored as the thallus. (HKL)

COMMENTS   Common on exposed cliffs and boulders, *Caloplaca trachyphylla* and *C. saxicola* are similar in appearance, but they lack apothecia. *Xanthoria fallax* has deep orange thalli and forms large colonies on deciduous trees.

Glossary

-aceae   suffix used to indicate the classification level of family

aethalia   the nonstalked spore case of slime molds

agaric   a fleshy mushroom bearing gills on the undersurface of the cap

-ales   suffix used to indicate the classification level of order

amyloid   staining grayish blue to blue-black in an iodine solution

annulus   the remains of a veil as a ring on the stalk

apothecia   the fruiting body of ascomycetes

ascus (asci)   sac-shaped cell that contains the spores of ascomycetes

basidium (basidia)   club-shaped cell on which the spores of basidiomycetes are borne

bolete   a fleshy mushroom bearing a tubelike layer on the undersurface of the cap

clavate   club-shaped; in a stalk, an enlargement at the basal end

columella   the sterile tissue that penetrates the gleba and is enclosed by the peridium (see also stalk-columella)

coniferous   trees which bear cones and have needlelike evergreen leaves

cortina   the cobwebby veil tissue of members of the Cortinariaceae

crustose   lichen growth form with the entire undersurface in contact with the substratum; colonies crustlike in appearance

deciduous   trees that annually lose their leaves as opposed to evergreen trees

decurrent   gills descending or running down the stalk

epigeous   growing or fruiting on or above the ground

fibril(-ose)   a fine hair; to be covered with fine hairs

foliose   a leaflike lichen growth form in which the margins of the thallus are unattached

fruiticose   a shrubby or hairlike lichen growth form

fungiphile   one who loves fungi; a mushroom hunter

genus   the first word in a species name

gills   in fungi, the fertile spore-bearing plates of an agaric; technically the lamellae

gleba   the fertile tissue and spore mass enclosed by a peridium; especially in gasteromycetes

hardwood   a broad-leaved tree

hymenium   a layer of spore-bearing cells, principally asci or basidia

hymenophore   the special tissue supporting an exposed hymenium, usually in the form of plates, tubes, branches, or spines

hyphae   the filamentous threads that constitute the body of a fungus

hypogeous   growing or fruiting below ground

lateral   attachment of the stalk to one side of the cap

latex   milk or juice that exudes from cut surfaces, as in *Lactarius*

lichens   cohabitation of a fungus with one or more algae, each deriving a benefit from the association

life zone   a region occupied by a characteristic group of plants, the boundary of which is determined by a particular combination of environmental conditions

molds   the asexual spore-producing states of a fungus

mutualistic symbionts   two different organisms living together, each deriving some benefit from the other, as in mycorrhizae and lichens

mycelium   the network of hyphae that make the body of a fungus

mycoflora   the collective inventory of fungus species in a particular area or region

mycophagist   one who eats fungi

mycorrhizae   the intimate association between a fungus and the rootlets of a tree *parasites* organisms that obtain their nutrition by feeding on another living organism

peridiole the small spore case of a bird's nest fungus

peridium wall surrounding a spore mass; a spore case

pileus the cap of a mushroom, which supports the hymenophore and the fertile cells

plasmodium the nonwalled, multinucleate, cytoplasmic body of a slime mold; the feeding stage of a slime mold

pores the open ends of tubes or cavities of fruiting bodies

primordium the early developmental stage of a mushroom; a young fruiting body before it has opened up

rhizines strands of hyphae on the lower surface of a lichen thallus

rhizomorph a threadlike or cordlike structure found at the base of mushrooms' fruiting bodies

saprophytes organisms that obtain their nutrition from dead organisms

scabers small brown to black tufts of hair or roughened tissue projecting from stalks, especially in *Leccinum*

scales small, flat pieces of tissue, aggregated together and often tapered to a pointed apex, usually of a different color than that of the surrounding tissue

scrobiculate having pitted spots on the surface of a stalk

species a single fungus type; the second word in a species name

sporangium a minute, stalked spore case produced by slime molds and molds

spore print a visible mass of spores deposited in a colored or uncolored pattern by the forceful release mechanisms of some fungi

spores the reproductive and dissemination unit of a fungus, usually a single cell

stalk the column of sterile tissue that supports the fertile spore-bearing tissue in a mushroom; technically a stipe

stalk-columella a stalklike column of sterile tissue that supports and penetrates the gleba and not totally enclosed by the peridium in the Agaricoid Gasteromycetes *striate*   having radial lines or furrows at the margin of the cap or along the stalk

tomentose   densely hairy or woolly

tubes   series of hollow cylinders open at one end and lined with basidia and spores in the polypores and boletes

veil   a thin layer of tissue: (a) *partial veil* connects the stalk to the edge of the cap and upon cap expansion leaves tissue on the cap margin or as a ring on the stalk; (b) *universal veil* covers a mushroom primordium and upon development of the stalk and cap leaves scales or patches of tissue on the cap and/or forms a cup at the base of the stalk in some mushrooms

viscid   sticky or slimy to the touch, usually from the production of mucus-like material

volva   remnant of the universal veil at the base of the stalk in the form of a cup, sheath, or collar

Bibliography

CROSS-REFERENCES

Arora, David. 1986. *Mushrooms Demystified: A Comprehensive Guide to the Fleshy Fungi.* 2d ed. Berkeley, California: Ten Speed Press.

Bessett, Alan, and Walter J. Sundberg. 1987. *Mushrooms: A Quick Reference Guide to Mushrooms of North America.* Macmillan Field Guides. New York: Macmillan Pub. Co.

Hale, Mason E. 1979. *How to Know Lichens.* 2d ed. The Pictured Key Nature Series. Dubuque, Iowa: Wm. C. Brown Co. Pub.

Lincoff, Gary H. 1981. *The Audubon Society Field Guide to North American Mushrooms.* New York: A. A. Knopf, Inc.

McKenny, Margaret, and Daniel E. Stuntz. 1987. *The New Savory Wild Mushroom.* Revised and enlarged by Joseph Ammirati. Seattle: University of Washington Press.

Miller, Orson K. 1977. *Mushrooms of North America.* Dubuque, Iowa: E. P. Dutton & Co.

Smith, Alexander H. 1975. *A Field Guide to the Western Mushrooms.* Ann Arbor: University of Michigan Press.

Smith, Alexander H., H. V. Smith, and Nancy S. Weber. 1979. *How to Know the Gilled Mushrooms.* The Pictured Key Nature Series. Dubuque, Iowa: Wm. C. Brown Co. Pub.

Smith, A. H., H. V. Smith, N. S. Weber. 1973. *How to Know the Non-Gilled Mushrooms.* The Pictured Key Nature Series. 2nd ed. Dubuque, Iowa: Wm. C. Brown. Co. Pub.

ADDITIONAL FIELD GUIDES

Gilbertson, Robert L., and L. Ryvarden. 1986. *North American Polypores.* Oslo: Fungiflora.

Guzman, Gaston. 1978. *Hongos.* Mexico City: Limusa.

McKnight, Kent H., and V. B. McKnight. 1987. *A Field Guide to Mushrooms of North America.* Boston: Houghton Mifflin Co.

Orr, Robert T., and D. B. Orr. 1979. *Mushrooms of Western North America.* California Natural History Guides, no. 42. Berkeley: University of California Press.

Smith, Alexander H., and N. S. Weber. 1980. *The Mushroom Hunters Field Guide.* Revised edition. Ann Arbor: University of Michigan Press.

Tylutki, Edward E. 1987. *Mushrooms of Idaho and the Pacific Northwest.* Vol. 2. *Non-gilled Hymenomycetes.* Moscow: University of Idaho Press.

SUGGESTED READING

Ammirati, Joseph F., J. A. Traquir, and P. A. Horgen. 1985. *Poisonous Mushrooms of the Northern United States and Canada.* Minneapolis: University of Minnesota Press.

Brown, David F., ed. 1982. *Biotic Communities of the American Southwest–United States and Mexico.* Special Issue: *Desert Plants* 4:1–4.

Lincoff, Gary, and D. H. Mitchel. 1977. *Toxic and Hallucinogenic Mushroom Poisoning.* New York: Van Nostrand Reinhold.

Stamets, Paul, and J. S. Chilton. 1983. *The Mushroom Cultivator: A Practical Guide to Growing Mushrooms at Home.* Olympia: Agarikon Press.

Index

Italicized page numbers refer
the reader to illustrations.

Abies. See Fir
  lasiocarpa. See Fir, subalpine
Acarospora
  chlorophana, 208, *209*
  schleicheri, 208
Agaricaceae, 43
  genera and species of, 107–10
Agaricales, 37, 42
  keys to, *31*, 42–43
Agaricus, 107, 155
  arvensis, 110
  brunnescens, 107, 145
  campestris, 107
  crocodilinus, 107
  hondensis, 109
  silvaticus, 109
  silvicola, 107, 109–10
  sp. (near *albolutescens*), 107, *108*
  xanthodermus, 110
Alder, 22, 181
Aleuria aurantia, 185
Alnus. See Alder
Alpine zone, 68
Amanita, 55, 147
  caesarea, 55–56
  calyptrata, 56
  gemmata, 56–57
  inaurata, 60
  muscaria, 57, 58, 59
  muscaria var. *formosa*, 59

  pantherina, 57, 58, 59
  pantherina-gemmata hybrid, 59,
    61
  rubescens, 59
  vaginata, 59–60, *61*
Amanitaceae (Amanitas), 43
  edibility of, 54–55
  genera and species of, 55–60
Amanitopsis, 55
  vaginata. See Amanita vaginata
Aphyllophorales, 41, 121–22
  coralloid, *34*, 38
  crustose, 38
  genera and species of, 125–42
  keys to, *34–35*, 123–24
  poroid, *35*, 37
  spinose, *34*, 38
Arcyria, 206
Arizona, 13, 16, 44, 54, 84
Armillaria, 81, 83
  albolanaripes, *82*, 83
  mellea. See Armillariella mellea
  ponderosa, 84
  straminea var. *americana*, *82*, 83
  zelleri, 83–84, *85*
Armillariella, 81
  mellea, 84, *85*
Artemisia. See Sagebrush
Artist's Conk, 130
Asci, 17

Ascomycetes, 17, 38, 171
  genera and species of, 173–85
  keys to, *30, 32,* 172, 187–89
  parasitization by, 69
  tuberlike, 36, 186–87
Aspen, 21
  Aphyllophorales with, 130, 135,
    138
  Ascomycetes with, 183
  Boletaceae with, 48
  Coprinaceae with, 104
  Gasteromycetes with, 152, 164
  Russulaceae with, 80
  Strophariaceae with, 112
  Tricholomataceae with, 83, 84,
    87, 88, 91, 95, 96
Asterophora, 81
Astreus, 164
  hygrometricus, 149, 164, *165*
Auricularia
  auricula, 142, *143,* 145
  mesenterica, 142
Auriculariales, *32,* 38, 142, 145

Baja California, 156
Balsamia magnata, 203
Basidia, 17
Basidiomycetes, 17, 41, 121
  keys to, *30,* 187–89
  tuberlike, 36, 147, 186–87
Battarrea
  digueti, 156
  phalloides, 148, 156, *157*
Bear's Head fungus, 135
Biotic communities. *See* Life zones
Bird's nest fungi, 146
  genera and species of, 160–63
Bisporella citrina, 185
Bjerkjandra adusta, 130
Bolbitiaceae, 101
Boletaceae (Boletes), 37, 41, 42, 44
  genera and species of, 45–54
  keys to, *35, 42*

Boletales, 42
Boletus, 44
  barrowsii, 45
  chrysenteron, 45, *46,* 47
  edulis, 45, *46,* 47
  zelleri, 47
Bracket fungus, 130
Brauniellula nancyae, 104, 148, *150,*
  151

Calbovista subsculpta, 149, 167–68
California, 56, 110, 145
Caloplaca
  saxicola, 214
  trachyphylla, 214
Calvatia
  booniana, 149, 168, *169,* 170
  craniiformis, 170
  cyathiformis, 169, 170
  fumosa, 168
  subcretacea, 168
Camarophyllus, 64
Canadian zone, 21
  Agaricaceae in, 110
  Amanitaceae in, *59,* 60
  Aphyllophorales in, 125, 126,
    130, 132, 135, 138, 141
  Ascomycetes in, 176, 183
  Boletaceae in, 47, 48, 49, 52
  Coprinaceae in, 104
  Cortinariaceae in, 114, 117
  Gasteromycetes in, 152, 164
  Gomphidiaceae in, 106
  Hygrophoraceae in, 66, 68
  jelly fungi in, 142, 145
  Lepiotaceae in, 65
  lichen in, 211
  Myxomycetes in, 206
  Russulaceae in, 73, 76
  Strophariaceae in, 112
  Tricholomataceae in, 83, 84, 87,
    91, 96

truffles and false truffles in, 193,
  196, 200, 203
Candelaria submexicana, 208, 209
Cantharellaceae, 37, 122, 125
  keys to, *31,* 123
Cantharellus cibarius, 26, 89, 122,
  123, *125*
Cedar, salt, 22, 156
Cep, 47
Chamonixia brevicolumna, 188,
  *189–*90
Chanterelles, 37, 41, 89, 122
  false, 125
  keys to, *31,* 123–24
  scaly, 122
  yellow, 122
Chaparral, 181
Chaparral Desert, 16
Chihuahuan Desert, 22
Chlamydopus, 156
Chlorophyllum molybdites, 60, 62
Chroogomphus, 104
  rutilus, 104
  vinicolor, 104, *105,* 151
Classification, 24–25
Clavaria
  purpurea, 123, 126, *127*
  vermicularis, 126
Clavariadelphus
  borealis, 123, 126, *127*
  ligula, 126
  pistillaris, 126
  truncatus, 126
Clavicorona pyxidata, 123, 126,
  128, 129
Clavulina cristata, 123, *128,* 129
Climate, fruiting, 19–21
Clitocybe, 81, 83
  *aurantiaca. See Hygrophoropsis
    aurantiaca*
  dilatata, 87
  gibba, 84, 86

gibba var. *maxima,* 86, *87*
  odora, 87
Club fungi, 17, 36, 41
Collection and identification, 23–24
Collybia, 83
Colorado, 13, 83, 84
Colorado Plateau, 52
Conifers, 13, 21
  Agaricaceae with, 109, 110
  Amanitaceae with, 57, 59
  Aphyllophorales with, 125, 126,
    129, 130, 132, 135, 136, 138,
    141, 142
  Ascomycetes with, 174, 176, 183
  Boletaceae with, 44, 47, 49, 51
  Cortinariaceae with, 112, 114,
    117
  Gasteromycetes with, 151, 162,
    164
  genera and species of, 19–22
  Gomphidiaceae with, 104, 106
  Hygrophoraceae with, 64, 66
  jelly fungi with, 142, 145
  Myxomycetes with, 206
  Pluteaceae with, 121
  Russulaceae with, 73, 74, 76, 80
  Strophariaceae with, 112
  Tricholomataceae with, 83, 84,
    87, 91, 93, 95, 97, 99, 100
  truffles and false truffles with, 41,
    193, 194, 196, 197, 200
Coprinaceae, 43
  genera and species of, 101–4
Coprinus, 101
  atramentarius, 101, *102,* 103
  comatus, 102, 103, 155
  micaceus, 103
Coral fungi, 38, 126
Coriolus versicolor, 124, *129–*30
Cortinariaceae, 43, 101, 112–13
  genera and species of, 113–20
Cortinarius, 112
  cedretorum, 114

gentilis, 114
   glaucopus group, *113–14*
   metarius group, 114, *115*
Cross-references, 27
Crucibulum laeve, 149, *160*
Crust fungi, 38, 122–23
Cultivated land, Coprinaceae in, 101
Cup fungi, *32,* 38, *171*
   genera and species of, 183–85
Cyathus
   stercorius, 161
   striatus, 148, *161*
Cystoderma, 81

Dacrymyces palmatus, 144, 145
Deciduous trees, 13
   Agaricaceae with, 110
   Aphyllophorales with, 126, 130,
      138
   Boletaceae with, 44, 47
   Gasteromycetes with, 156, 161
   genera and species of, 19–22
   lichens with, 214
   Myxomycetes with, 206
   Pluteaceae with, 121
   Tricholomataceae with, 96
   truffles with, 194
   See also Hardwoods
Dentinum, 122
Deserts, 22, 155, 156, 159
Discina perlata, 183
Douglas Fir, 21, 52, 59, 64, 74, 89,
      91, 106, 132, 138, 183, 203
Dung
   Coprinaceae on, 101
   Gasteromycetes on, 161
   Strophariaceae on, 111, 112

Earthstars, 146
   genera and species of, 164–70
Elaphomyces, 172, 187, 188
   granulatus, 190, *191*

Endoptychum
   agaricoides, 152
   arizonicum, 152
   depressum, 151–52
Entoloma, 120
Entolomataceae, 43, 120

Fairy rings, 129
False Shaggy Mane, 155
Feeding bodies, 16
Fir
   Amanitaceae with, 57, 59, 60
   Aphyllophorales with, 126, 130,
      132, 138, 142
   Ascomycetes with, 176, 183
   Boletaceae with, 49, 52
   Gomphidiaceae with, 106
   Hygrophoraceae with, 66
   Lepiotaceae with, 64
   lichen with, 211
   Russulaceae with, 74
   subalpine, 21, 106, 130, 190
   Tricholomataceae with, 89, 91, 99
   truffles and false truffles with, 190,
      203
   See also Douglas Fir
Flammulina velutipes, 87–88
Floccularia albolinaripes. See
      Armillaria albolanaripes
Fomes pinicola, 130
Fomitopsis
   pinicola, 124, 130, *131*
   subrosea, 130
Forests, 13, 170. *See also* Conifers;
      Deciduous trees; Hardwoods
Fruiting, climatic conditions for,
      19–21
Fruiting bodies, collection of, 23–24
Fuligo
   megaspora, 206
   septica, 204, *205,* 206
Fungi
   bear's head, 135

bracket, 130
classification of, 24–25
club, 17, 36, 41
collection of, 23–24
coral, 38, 126
crust, 38, 122–23
edibility of, 18–19
epigeous, 186
growth of, 17–18
hallucinogenic, 19
hedgehog, 135
hypogeous, 187, 188
nutrition of, 16–17
poisonous, 18–19
saddle, 171
teeth, *34*, 38
tuberlike, 172
See also Bird's nest fungi; Cup
   fungi; Jelly fungi; Molds, slime;
   Mushrooms; Sac fungi; Stomach fungi; Truffles

Ganoderma applanatum, 124, 130,
   131
Gasteromycetes, 36, 41, 122
   agaricoid, *32*, 37, 41, 146–47
   genera and species of, 150–70
   keys to, *33*, 147–49
   stomach fungi, 41
Gautieria, 188
   crispa, 190, *192,* 193
   gautieroides, 190, *191*
   monticola, 190
Geastrum, 149
   fimbriatum, 164, *165*
   fornicatum, 166, 167
   mammosum, 167
   minimum, 167
   rufescens, 167
   saccatum, 164
   triplex, 164
   xerophilum, 167
Genabea, 193–94

Genaea, 193–94
Geode truffles, 193–94
Geopora cooperi, 187, *192,* 193–94
Gloeophyllum sepiarium, 124, *132*
Gomphidiaceae, 43
   genera and species of, 104–6
Gomphidius
   glutinosus, 104, *105,* 106
   subroseus, 106
Gomphus
   floccosus, 122, 123, 132, *133*
   kauffmanii, 122, 123, *134,* 135
Grasslands, 13, 22, 107, 159
Great Basin Desert, 22, 156, 213
Great Plains, 13
Gueopiniopsis alpinus, 145
Gymnopilus, 112, 113
   sapineus, 114
   spectabilis, 114, *115*
Gyromitra spp., 172, 181
   esculenta, 173
   gigas, 173
   infula, 174
Gyrophragmium. See Endoptychum
   depressum
Gyroporus, 44

Hardwoods
   Aphyllophorales with, 126, 130,
      135, 138, 141
   Ascomycetes with, 174, 176, 179,
      181, 183
   Cortinariaceae with, 114, 119
   Gasteromycetes with, 161, 162
   Strophariaceae with, 112
   Tricholomataceae with, 84, 87, 99
   See also Deciduous trees
Hebeloma, 112
   crustuliniforme, 114, *116,* 117
   insigne, 116, 117
   sinapizans, 117
Hedgehog fungus, 135

Helotium citrinum. See Bisporella citrina
Helvella, 172
  acetabulum, 172, 174, *175,* 183
  compressa, 176
  crispa, 176
  lacunosa, 176
Hemitrichia, 206
Hericium
  abietis, 135
  erinaceum, 124, *134,* 135
  ramosum, 135
Hirschioporus abietinum. See Trichaptum abietinum
Honey mushroom, 84
Host plants, 13
Hudsonian zone, 21
  Agaricaceae in, 110
  Amanitacae in, 60
  Aphyllophorales in, 126, 135, 141
  Ascomycetes in, 176
  Boletaceae in, 47, 49
  Cortinariaceae in, 114
  Gasteromycetes in, 164, 168
  Gomphidiaceae in, 106
  Hygrophoraceae in, 66
  jelly fungi in, 142, 145
  lichen in, 211
  Myxomycetes in, 206
  Russulaceae in, 73, 74, 76, 80
  Tricholomataceae in, 84, 87, 96
  truffles and false truffles in, 190, 193, 196, 200
Hydnaceae, 122
Hydnellum, 122
  scrobiculatum group, 124, 135, *136*
Hydnotrya, 193
  cerebriformis, 193
  variiformis, 193
Hydnum, 122
  imbricatum, 124, 136, *137*
  ramosum, 136

Hygrocybe, 64
Hygrophoraceae, 43
  genera and species of, 64–68
Hygrophoropsis, 83
  aurantiaca, 26, 88–89, 125
Hygrophorus, 89, 106
  chrysodon, 64, 65
  conicus, 68
  eburneus, 64, 68
  erubescens, 64, 65, 66
  hypothejus, 67
  pudorinus, 66
  russula, 66
  speciosus, 67
  subalpinus, 68
Hymenogaster
  parksii, 194
  sublilacinus, 188, 194, *195*
Hyphae, 16
Hypomyces, 69, 171, 172, 177
  lactifluorum, 177, 179
  luteovirens, 178, 179
Hysterangium, 188, 194
  coriaceum, 194
  separabile, 194, *195*

Identification, 23–24
Inky Caps, 101
Inocybe, 112
  geophylla var. *lilacina,* 117, *118*

Jelly fungi, *32, 38,* 142
  genera and species of, 142–45
Juniper, 21
  Gasteromycetes with, 159, 160, 167
  Russulaceae with, 70
Juniperus. See Juniper

Keys
  to Agaricales, 42–43
  to Aphyllophorales, 123–24
  to Ascomycetes, 172, 187–89

to Basidiomycetes, 187–89
to Boletaceae, 42
to Gasteromycetes, 147–49
to Myxomycetes, 37
narrative, 25–26, 36–38
picture, 26, 30–35
to sac fungi, 172
to truffles, 187–89
King Bolete, 47

Laccaria
  amethystina, 91
  laccata, 89, 90, 91
  Lactarius, 68, 69, 71, 177
  alnicola group, 69–70, 72
  barrowsii, 70, 71
  deliciosus, 72, 73
  indigo, 72, 73
  parasites of, 177
  representaneus, 73–74
  rubrilacteus, 73, 74, 75
  rufus, 75, 76
  sanguifluus, 74
  scrobiculatus, 70
  sp. (near *chelidonium*), 70, 71, 73
  uvidus, 76, 77
Leccinum, 44
  aurantiacum, 48
  insigne, 47–48
  montanum, 48
  subalpinum, 48–49
Lentinellus ursinus, 91, 96
Lentinus, 81
  lepideus, 91
  ponderosus, 90, 91
Lepiota
  clypeolaria, 62, 63, 64
  lutea, 60
  racodes, 62
Lepiotaceae (Lepiotas), 43, 60
  genera and species of, 62–64
Leptoglossum, 81
Leptonia, 120

Leucogaster, 189
  rubescens, 196
Leucopaxillus, 81, 83
  albissimus, 91, 92, 93
  amarus, 91, 92, 93
  gentianeus, 93
Leucophleps, 189
  spinospora, 196
Lichens, 12, 16
  crustose, 207
  foliose, 207, 208, 211, 213
  fruiticose, 207, 211
  keys to, *30, 36*
Life zones, 12, 19–22
Limacella, 55
  glishra, 60
Lobster Mushroom, 177
Longula texensis, 148, 152, *153,*
  155
Lower Montane zone. *See* Transition
  zone
Lower Sonoran zone, 21, 22
Lycogala epidendrum, 206
Lycoperdon spp., 149, 162
  perlatum, 166, 167
  pyriforme, 167
Lyophyllum, 81

Macrolepiota racodes. See Lepiota
  racodes
Marasmius, 83
Matsutake, 84
Melanogaster tuberiformis, 189,
  196–97
Melanoleuca, 81
Mexico, 13, 54, 84, 156, 199
Mohave Desert, 22
Molds, slime, 17, 37, 204–6
Montagnea arenarius, 148, *154,* 155
Montagnites. See Montagnea
  arenarius
Morchella, 172
  angusticeps, 179

conica, 179
deliciosa group, *178,* 179
elata, 179, *180,* 181
esculenta, 20, *181*
Morchellaceae, 171
Morels, *32, 38*
  black, 179
  edibility of, 171, 179
  false, 171, 173, 174
  white, 179
  yellow, 179, 181
Mountains, 13, 142. *See also various
    life zones*
Mushrooms
  as dye source, 138
  edibility of, 18–19, 44
  edibility questioned or unknown,
    56, 57, 60, 64, 69, 73, 78, 93,
    99, 100, 104, 107, 119, 125,
    132, 135, 141, 142, 151, 155,
    159, 162, 173, 174, 177, 183
  edible, 45, 47, 48, 49, 51, 52, 54,
    59, 60, 66, 73, 74, 78, 83, 84,
    86, 87, 88, 89, 91, 96, 100,
    101, 103, 106, 109, 110, 122,
    126, 135, 136, 142, 145, 167,
    168, 170, 171, 179, 183
  fleshy, *31,* 41, 42–43
  fleshy gilled, 42
  fleshy pored, *35,* 37, 42, 44
  growth of, 17–18
  hallucinogenic, 19, 101, 111
  honey, 84
  inedible, 78, 91, 95, 96, 99, 114,
    130, 135, 138, 145, 147, 162
  lobster, 177
  oyster, 96
  poisonous, 18–19, 54–55, 59, 60,
    62, 64, 70, 74, 76, 80, 87, 88,
    94, 97, 101, 107, 111, 113,
    114, 117, 120, 171, 174, 179
  snow, 173
  See also Fungi; Puffballs; Truffles

Mycelium, 16, 17
Mycena, 83, 94
  alcalina, 93
  pura, 94
Mycorrhizae, 17
  Cortinariaceae as, 112, 117
  Gomphidiaceae as, 104
  and host associates, 13, 16
  truffles as, 186, 203
Myxomycetes, 17, 204–6
  keys to, *33,* 37

Naematoloma, 110–11
New Mexico, 13, 16, 44, 54, 83, 84,
  107
Nolanea, 120

Oak, 21, 22
  Aphyllophorales with, 126, 130,
    135
  Ascomycetes with, 183
  Gasteromycetes with, 170
  Hygrophoraceae with, 66, 68
  Russulaceae with, 73
  Tricholomataceae with, 84, 86, 93
  truffles with, 194, 203
Omphalina, 81
Omphalotus, 81
Otidea
  alutacea, 183
  leporina, 172, *182,* 183
Oyster mushroom, 96

Panaeolus, 101
  campanulatus, 101
  foenisecii, 101
Panellus, 81, 95
*Panellus nidulans. See Phyllotopsis
    nidulans*
Panus, 81
Parasites, 16, 17, 69, 177
Parmelia spp., 211

Paxina acetabulum. See Helvella
  acetabulum
Peltigera
  maleacea, 208, *210*
  polydactyla, 208
Peridium, 18, 146
Pezizaceae, 171
Peziza repanda, 172, 182, 183
Phaeolus schweinitzii, 124, 136,
  137, 138
Phallus impudicus, 148, 156, *158,*
  181
Phellinus tremulae, 124, 138, *139*
Phellorina strobilina, 156
Phlogiotis helvelloides, 145
Pholiota, 112, 113
  albocrenulata, 120
  squarrosa, 118, 119
  terrestris, 119, 120
Phyllotopsis, 81, 83
  nidulans, 95
Physcia caesia, 208, *210*
Picea. See Spruce
Pine
  Aphyllophorales with, 125, 126,
    129, 130, 132, 136, 138
  Ascomycetes with, 183
  Boletaceae with, 48, 49, 51, 52
  bristlecone, 21, 76
  Cortinariaceae with, 114
  Gastromycetes with, 151, 152,
    159, 160, 162, 167
  Gomphidiaceae with, 104, 106
  Hygrophoraceae with, 64, 67, 68
  Lepiotaceae with, 64
  limber, 21, 132
  lodgepole, 21, 104, 190, 193, 197,
    200
  pinyon, 21, 70, 97, 159, 160, 167,
    200
  ponderosa, 21, 45, 52, 55, 59, 64,
    67, 70, 76, 91, 104, 106, 114,

138, 152, 190, 193, 197, 200,
    201, 203
  Russulaceae with, 70, 73, 76, 78,
    80
  Tricholomataceae with, 84, 86,
    91, 93, 96, 97, 99
  truffles and false truffles with, 190,
    193, 197, 199, 200, 203
  white, 49, 200
Pink Crown, 183
Pinus. See Pine
  aristata. See Pine, bristlecone
  contorta. See Pine, lodgepole
  edulis. See Pine, pinyon
  flexilis. See Pine, limber
  ponderosa. See Pine, ponderosa
Plasmodium, 17
Pleurotus, 81, 83
  elongatipes, 96
  nidulans. See Phyllotopsis
    nidulans
  ostreatus, 95–96
Pluteaceae, 43, 120
  genera and species of, 120–21
Pluteus
  atromarginatus, 121
  cervinus, 121
  lutescens, 120–21
Podaxis pistillaris, 148, *154, 155*
Polypores, *35,* 37, 38, 41, 122
Polyporus
  adusta. See Bjerkjandra adusta
  schweinitzii. See Phaeolus
    schweinitzii
  versicolor. See Coriolus versicolor
Poplar, 181
Populus tremuloides. See Aspen
Precipitation, 19
Primordium, 16
Psathyrella, 101
  circellatipes, 103–4
  hydrophylla, 104
Pseudevernia intensa, 211

Pseudohydnum gelatinosum, 145
Pseudotsuga menzesii. *See* Fir,
    Douglas
Psilocybe, 110, 111
    coprophila, 112
Puffballs, 18, 36, 41
    edible, 147, 167, 168, 170
    giant, 168–70
    hard-skinned, 147, 162, 164
    narrative key, 36, 147–49
    soft-skinned, 162
    stalked, 146, 151, 156–59
Pycnoporellus
    alboluteus, 124, 138, *139*
    cinnabarinus, 138

Quercus. *See* Oak

Radiigera atrogleba, 147, *150, 151,*
    188
Ramaria
    flava, 142
    formosa group, 124, *140,* 141
    rasilispora group, 124, *141*–42
    sanguinea, 142
    stricta, 126
Rhizomorphs, 16
Rhizoplaca chrysoleuca, 208, *209*
Rhizopogon, 189, 203
    evadens, 197, *198*
    fallax, 200
    occidentalis, 199
    ochraceorubens, *198*, 199
    pinyonensis, 199–200
    rubescens, 197
    subcaerulescens, *200*
Rhodophyllaceae. *See*
    Entolomataceae
Riparian zone, 13, 22
    Aphyllophorales in, 130, 135,
        138, 141
    Ascomycetes in, 179, 181
    Boletaceae in, 44, 47, 48

Gasteromycetes in, 156, 162, 170
Strophariaceae in, 112
Tricholomataceae in, 96, 99
truffles in, 194, 203
Roadways, 103, 120, 164
Russula, 68, 69, 177, 179
    aeruginea, 80
    albonigra, 78
    alutacea group, 76, 77, 78
    brevipes, 69, 72, 78, 79
    claroflava, 80
    delica, 78
    emetica, 78, 79, 80
    luculentus, 76
    maculata group, 78
    nigricans, 78
    parasites of, 177, 179
    rosacea, 80, *81*
    sanguineus, 80
    xerampelina, 80
Russulaceae (Russulas), 43, 68–69
    genera and species of, 69–80

Sac fungi, 17, 171
    genera and species of, 173–85
    keys to, *32*, 172
    parasitic, *32*, 38
Saddle fungi, 171
Sagebrush, 21, 22, 52, 170
Saprophytes, 16, 17, 94
Sarcoscypha coccinea, 185
Sarcosphaera, 171
    coronaria, 183
    crassa, 172, 183, *184*
    exima, 183
Scleroderma
    aurantiacum, 162
    citrinum, 162
    hypogaeum, 149, 161, *162*
    michiganense, 149, 162, *163*
Sclerogaster xerophilum, 188, *201*
Scrubland, 22
Sculptured Puffball, 168

Scutellinia scutellata, 172, *184, 185*
Secotium. See Endoptychum
   depressum
Shadscale, 22
Shaggy Mane, 103
Snowbanks, mushrooms found near,
   21, 68, 145, 173
Snowberry, 21
Snow mushroom, 173
Sonoran Desert, 22, 206
Sonoran zone, 21, 22
Sparassis
   crispa, 123, 142, *143*
   radicata, 142
Spathularia flavida, 126
Spore prints, 17, 24
Spores, 16
Spruce, 21
   Amanitaceae with, 57, 60
   Aphyllophorales with, 126, 142
   Ascomycetes with, 176
   Boletaceae with, 49
   false truffles with, 190
   Gomphidiaceae with, 106
   Hygrophoraceae with, 66, 67
   lichen with, 211
   Russulaceae with, 74, 76
Stemonitis, 206
Stereaceae, 123
Stinkhorns, 146, 151, 156, 181
Stomach fungi, 41, 122, 146
   genera and species of, 150–70
   keys to, *33,* 147–49
Strobilomyces, 44
Stropharia, 110
   coronilla, 112
   kauffmanii, 111–12
   riparia, 112
   semiglobata, 112
Strophariaceae, 43, 110–11
   genera and species of, 111–12
Subalpine zone. *See* Hudsonian zone
Suillus, 44

albidipes, 51
americanus, 49, 50, 51
brevipes, 50, 51
granulatus, 51–52
kaibabensis, 52
lakei, 52, 53
pseudobrevipes, 52
sibiricus, 49, 52, *53*
tomentosus, 54
Sycamore, 181
Symbionts, mutualistic, 16

Tamarisk chinensis. See Cedar, salt
Teeth fungi, *34, 38*
Temperature, 19
Texas, 13
Thelephoraceae, 123
Trametes, 130
Trametes versicolor. See Coriolus
   versicolor
Transition zone, 21
   Amanitaceae in, 60
   Aphyllophorales in, 125, 129, 138
   Ascomycetes in, 183
   Boletaceae in, 45, 48
   Coprinaceae in, 104
   Cortinariaceae in, 114, 117
   Gasteromycetes in, 151, 152, 164
   Gomphidiaceae in, 106
   Hygrophoraceae in, 68
   Lepiotaceae in, 64
   lichens in, 213
   Myxomycetes in, 206
   Russulaceae in, 73, 80
   Tricholomataceae in, 84, 86, 97
   truffles and false truffles in, 190,
      193, 197, 199, 201
Tremellales, 32, 38, 142
Tremella mesenterica, 145
Trichaptum abietinum, 130
Trichia, 206
Tricholoma, 81

magnivelare. See Armillaria
  ponderosa
pardinum, 96–97
saponaceum, 97, *98, 99*
terreum, 97
zelleri. See Armillaria zelleri
Tricholomataceae, 43, 80–81, 83
  genera and species of, 83–100
Tricholomopsis
  platyphylla, 98, 99
  rutilans, 99–100
Trogia, 81
Truffles, 11, 18, 171
  edibility unknown or questioned,
    190, 193, 203
  edible, 186, 203
  false, *30*, 36, 41, 147, 187, 197,
    199, 201, 203
  geode, 193–94
  inedible, 194
  keys to, *30, 36*, 187–89
  See also Ascomycetes, tuberlike;
    Basidomycetes, tuberlike
Truncocolumella citrina, 188, 201,
  202, 203
Tuber, 186–87
  dryophilum, 203
  gibbosum, 203
  levissimum, 188, *202*, 203
  rufum, 203
Tuberales, 186
Tulostoma, 156
  brumale, 159
  cretaceum, 159
  opacum, 159
  poculatum, 159
  simulans, 159
  striatum, 159
Turkey Tail, 130
Tylopilus, 44

Upper Montane zone. *See* Canadian
  zone
Upper Sonoran zone, 21
  Amanitaceae in, 60
  Ascomycetes in, 181
  Gasteromycetes in, 159, 164
  lichens in, 213
  Russulaceae in, 80
  truffles and false truffles in, 200,
    201
Usnea, 211
  arizonica, 211, *212, 213*
  cavernosa, 213
  hirta, 213
Utah, 13

Vegetational zones, 14–15 (map),
  21. *See also* Life zones
Veil, 18
Verpa, 179
  bohemica, 181
Volvariaceae. *See* Pluteaceae
Volvariella, 120

Western Giant Puffball, 170
Wood ear, 145
Woodlands, 13. *See also* Conifers;
  Deciduous trees; Hardwoods;
  Riparian zone

Xanthoparmelia
  chlorochroa, 213
  lineola, 213
Xanthoria
  elegans, 214
  fallax, 214
Xerocomus chrysenteron. See
  Boletus chrysenteron
Xeromphalina campanella, 100

Photograph Credits

DAVID ARORA

Lactarius barrowsii, 71
Lactarius indigo, 72
Armillaria albolinaripes, 82
Pleurotus ostreatus, 96
Endoptychum depressum, 152

ROBERT CHAPMAN

Hygrophorus erubescens, 65
Hygrophorus speciosus, 67
Lactarius alnicola, 69
Lactarius uvidus, 77
Russula brevipes, 79
Armillaria straminea, 82
Hebeloma crustuliniforme, 116
Gomphus floccosus, 133
Phaeolus schweinitzii, 137
Sparrasis crispa, 143
Longula texensis, 153

ROBERT GILBERTSON

Russula rosacea, 81
Tricholomopsis platyphylla, 98

CAROL LANPHEAR-COOK

Gyromitra infula, 174

JOHN MENGE

Boletus chrysenteron, 46
Chlorophyllum molybdites, 62
Coriolus versicolor, 129
Ramaria formosa, 140
Crucibulum laeve, 160

Geastrum fornicatum, 166
Helvella acetabulum, 175
Morchella elata, 180
Otidea leporina, 182
Sarcosphaera crassa, 184
Scutellinia scutellata, 184

THOMAS H. NASH III

Physcia caesia, 210
Xanthoria elegans, 214

CLARK SCHAAK

Russula emetica, 79

WALTER SUNDBERG

Inocybe lilacina, 118
Melanogaster tuberiformis, 197
Gomphidius subroseus, 106
Xeromphalina campanella, 100

GREG WRIGHT

Boletus edulis, 46
Clitocybe gibba, 86
Flammulina velutipes, 88
Laccaria laccata, 90
Tricholoma pardinum, 97
Agaricus silvicola, 110
Cantharellus cibarius, 125
Montagnea arenarius, 154
Astreus hygrometricus, 165
Geopora cooperi, 192
Morchella esculenta, 181

About the Author

Jack S. States has been on the faculty of the Department of Biology at Northern Arizona University, Flagstaff, since 1970. In 1969 he received a doctorate in botany-mycology from the University of Alberta. Since then he has been a contributor to professional publications such as *Mycotaxon* and *Mycologia*. He has lectured and conducted workshops on mycological topics to both professional and amateur groups such as the Audobon Society, the Los Angeles Mycological Society, and the San Francisco Mycological Society. He has been a member of the Mycological Society of America since 1966.

His ongoing research interests include the ecology of mycorrhizal fungi associated with conifers, and the systematics and ecology of truffles and false truffles of the Southwest.

Ruler for measuring mushroom specimens and for converting centimeters to inches